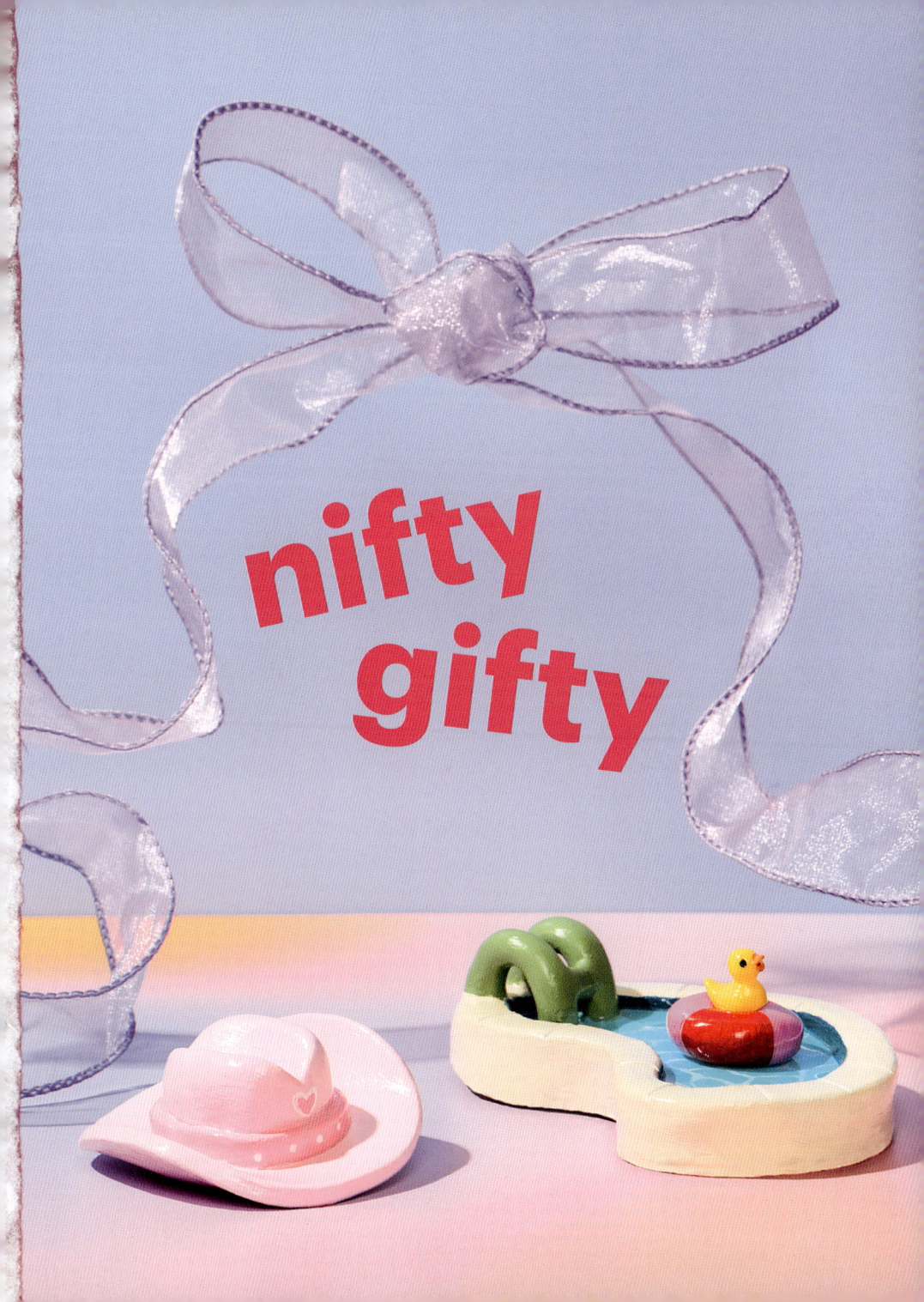

ALEXA PEDRERO
photography by ANDRIA LO

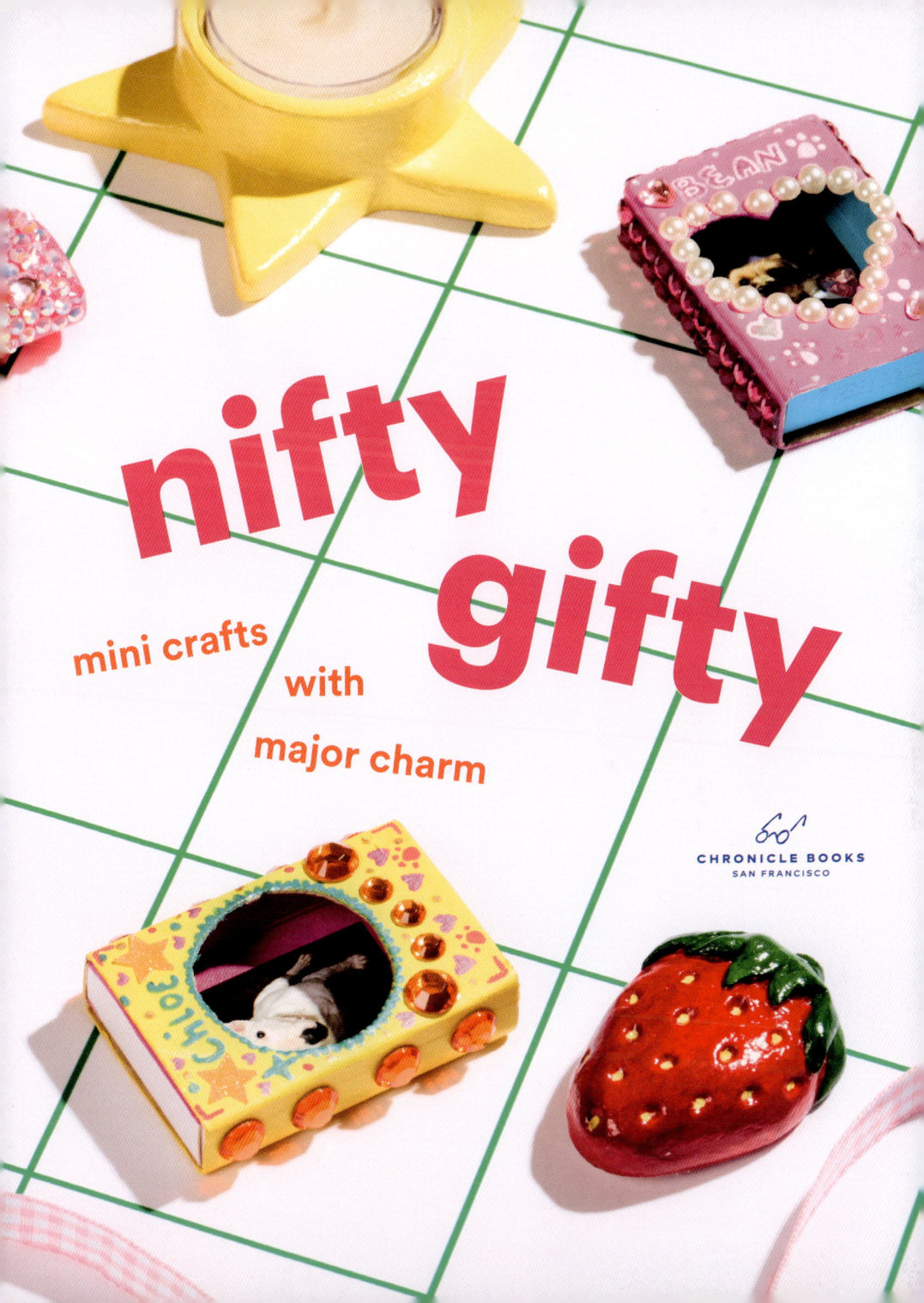

# nifty gifty

mini crafts with major charm

CHRONICLE BOOKS
SAN FRANCISCO

Text copyright © 2025 by Alexa Pedrero.
Photographs copyright © 2025 by
Chronicle Books LLC.

All rights reserved. No part of this book
may be reproduced in any form without
written permission from the publisher.

Library of Congress Cataloging-in-
Publication Data available.

ISBN 978-1-7972-3163-1

Manufactured in China.

MIX
Paper | Supporting
responsible forestry
FSC™ C104723

Photography and prop styling by Andria Lo.
Design by Rachel Harrell and
Wynne Au-Yeung.

10 9 8 7 6 5 4 3 2 1

Chronicle books and gifts are available
at special quantity discounts to corpora-
tions, professional associations, literacy
programs, and other organizations. For
details and discount information, please
contact our premiums department at
corporatesales@chroniclebooks.com
or at 1-800-759-0190.

Chronicle Books LLC
680 Second Street
San Francisco, California 94107
www.chroniclebooks.com

# CONTENTS

Introduction 8

Crafter's Toolbox 10

Mushroom Picture Holder 22

Juice Box Picture Holder 28

Mini Trinket Shelf 36

Strawberry Trinket Dish 40

Mini Pool-Shaped Trinket Dish 44

Bejeweled Lighter 52

Mint Tin Wallet 58

Funky Bookmarks 62

Eraser Stamp 70

Fruit Magnets 74

Cowboy Boot Matchbox with Cowboy Hat Striker 82

Sun Incense Holder 88

Sardine Tin Toothpick Holder 92

Star Tealight Candle Holder 98

Vintage Magazine Collage Frame 102

Collage Memory Board 106

Embroidered Bag Charm 110

Beaded Lampshade 118

Matchbox Shrine 122

Fake Cake Gift Box 126

Acknowledgments 134

About the Author 137

Index 138

# Introduction

Being crafty has been a part of my identity for as long as I can remember. It has become a crucial part of who I am as an artist and as a person overall. I like to believe that I possess the "How hard can it be?" gene in my DNA. This particular trait has made me think that I can build, make, or create anything I set my mind to.

In addition to my love for creating, there has always been something else that I love equally: gift giving. Ever since I combined these two passions, it has opened up countless creative opportunities in my life, and for that I will be forever grateful.

In 2020 I decided to post and share many of my crafting methods online, and to my surprise, people really liked my videos. They would comment things like, "Time to start a new hobby," or "I can't wait to make this." Seeing that thousands of people would get inspired by my sometimes silly creations inspired me to create even more! It was like a never-ending inspiration cycle.

With this nifty little crafting book, I'd love to inspire even more people to create sweet, charming, and unique gifts. Throughout the book, I'll guide you step-by-step on my creation process for gift making and gift giving to give *you*, the reader, an opportunity to be inspired to make giftable crafts and maybe turn that into a passion of your own.

I believe that creativity is a gift that everyone has. You may think you don't have a single creative bone in your body, but you do! Making handmade gifts is a fun and unique way to nurture the creative part of your brain while bringing joy to the person they're intended for!

# Crafter's Toolbox

Here's a quick guide of all the supplies you'll need to create the gifts in this book.

**ADHESIVES**

### Craft glue
A simple and effective way to adhere paper or other lightweight objects to one another.

### Glue stick
A compact alternative to craft glue for lightweight objects.

### Masking tape
Use for creating clean lines or masking areas when painting. It's removable and doesn't damage the work surface.

### Strong silicone glue (like E6000)
Ideal for adhering heavier objects to one another. It's waterproof and is extra durable for any 3D decorating.

## BEADING

### Beading wire
A durable way to string beads. Comes in multiple gauges.

### Beads
The best kind of beads for your collection are glass, stone, and wooden beads.

### Embroidery needle
For adding beads and colorful thread to felt and other materials.

### Pliers
Ideal for wrapping wire in tight loops for a durable hold.

### Wire cutters
Ideal for cutting wire with ease.

cont'd →

## CLAY

### Air-dry clay

Perfect for when you want to create something ceramic-like without the hassle of a kiln.
I would recommend purchasing light-colored clay so you don't have to prime your creations before painting it different colors.

## BASIC CLAY TOOLS

### Canvas mat

Helps prevent clay from sticking to the surface during the sculpting process.

### Clay blade

A long, thin, and flat metal blade. Ideal for cutting clay in clean and even shapes.

### Clay sponge

Perfect for smoothing the surface of the clay.

### Dotting tool

Great for creating texture and small details on clay figures.

### Fettling knife (also known as a wooden clay knife)
A multifunctional tool that works great for slicing, smoothing, and scoring clay.

### Flat sculpting tool
Perfect for creating sharp edges.

### Loop tool
Helps to carve out unnecessary clay while sculpting.

### Needle tool
Use for scoring smaller pieces of clay. Can also be used to cut or slice.

### Plastic or acrylic rolling pin
Best nonstick option for rolling out clay.

### Rounded sculpting tool
Perfect for creating smooth rounded edges.

### Silicone tip sculpting tool
Ideal for creating small and intricate details and texture on small clay figures.

cont'd →

### DECORATION

#### Embellishments
Buttons, ribbons, rhinestones, scrapbook paper, and stickers can all be used to make your crafts extremely personal to you or to whoever will be receiving it.

### MARKERS/PENS

#### Assortment of colorful water-based markers
Useful for outlining, drawing, and adding colorful details to any project.

### MULTIMEDIA HANDY SUPPLIES

#### Mixed media paper
Extra-thick paper that can be painted on without losing its shape due to moisture.

#### Ruler
Ideal for drawing or cutting straight edges and measuring the size of crafts.

#### Tweezers
Use to place small beads or decorative elements onto glue or hard-to-reach areas.

cont'd →

### PAINTING

#### Acrylic paint
Beginner-friendly paint that can be used for clay, canvas, wood, and glass.

#### Medium and small flat-head paintbrushes
Great for covering large areas with paint. Also good for creating clean edges and lines.

#### Medium and small round-edge paintbrushes
Ideal for details like creating texture or organic shapes with paint.

#### Small disposable plastic or paper cups
Great for mixing and storing custom mixed paints and dyed spackling.

**SCISSORS/CUTTING SUPPLIES**

### Regular sharp scissors

Used for cutting paper, fabric, and a wide variety of other materials.

### X-Acto knife

Small multipurpose blade that is ideal for cutting smaller objects.

**SEALANTS**

### Acrylic varnish

A durable and glossy coat to preserve your crafts while giving them a shiny finish.

### Clear, paper-safe sealant spray (like Mod Podge)

Easy-apply glossy coat alternative. Great for larger crafts.

### UV resin and UV resin curing lamp (optional)

A very durable high-gloss sealant that cures under a UV lamp.

# Mushroom Picture Holder

**CRAFTING TIME: 15-20 MINUTES**

**SUPPLIES**

You know how mushrooms need specific growing conditions but can also pop up in the most unexpected places? I think creativity is kind of like that. Inspiration can appear when you least expect it, and a random idea can grow into something beautiful.

This craft was inspired by that concept (but also, and more importantly, by the fact that mushrooms are cute). Let's use this little mushroom as a symbol of new beginnings and the start of our wonderful gift-making journey together.

Also, you do not have to follow the size suggestions in the instructions. They are there just in case you want to make it *exactly* like mine. You are more than welcome to make your lil mushie as big or small as you'd like.

**Canvas mat (optional)**

**½ lb [230 g] air-dry clay**

**Clay blade**

**Scoring and slipping tools (see page 34), preferably a fettling knife**

**Medium round-edge paintbrush**

**Small flat-head paintbrush**

**Acrylic paint (I recommend beige, red, and white)**

**Acrylic varnish**

1. On a canvas mat or a clean and flat surface, roll the clay into a ball about 2 in [5 cm] in diameter. Using the clay blade, slice the clay ball into two even halves.

2. Take one of the halves and roll it into a ball. This one will be for the stem or base of the mushroom. Roll out the clay ball until it starts to look like a chubby coil and taper one side into a cone shape. This will be the top of the stem where you'll join it to the mushroom cap.

**3** Now grab the other clay half. Stick your thumb into the center of the flat side of the clay and gently pinch and stretch the clay around the imprint to create a bowl shape for the top of the mushroom.

With a fettling knife, score the underside of the mushroom top and top of the base (see page 34). Slip and join the mushroom top and base. Using the clay tool of your choice, blend and smooth the clay as needed. Join the mushroom cap and stem together.

**4** Using the clay blade, create a small, 1 in [2.5 cm] slice at the top of the mushroom to leave a notch where pictures can be placed once this mushroom is painted and varnished. Set the mushroom aside to dry. Drying times vary, so follow the suggestions on the package of clay.

cont'd →

**5** Once the mushroom is completely dry, it's ready to be painted! For a traditional look, I recommend painting the stem and inside of the mushroom cap a beige color, painting the top of the mushroom cap a bright red, and adding white dots.

After the paint is dry, brush the mushroom with a light coat of acrylic varnish to make your project more durable.

> If you're not feeling the traditional colors, you can paint your mushie any color you like! You can make a whole army of these little guys and gift them to your friends so you all have matching picture holders with slight color variations that match their aesthetics. Painting the top of your mushroom pink with white dots gives it a flower fairy vibe, whereas painting it black with white dots is more of a gothic take.

NIFTY GIFTY

# Juice Box Picture Holder

**CRAFTING TIME: 30-45 MINUTES**

What better way to keep creative juices flowing than to create a juice box picture holder? This picture holder variation is perfect for anyone who likes to decorate their space with cute and quirky foodie decor. But let's be honest, who doesn't want a treasured picture housed atop a sweet lil juice box?

**SUPPLIES**

Canvas mat (optional)

Plastic or acrylic rolling pin

½ lb [230 g] air-dry clay

Scoring and slipping tools (see page 34), preferably an X-Acto knife

Rounded sculpting tool

Clay sponge

Clay blade

Small plastic bendy straw

Paintbrushes

Acrylic paint

Acrylic varnish

**1** On a canvas mat or a clean and flat surface, use the rolling pin to roll the clay out to a ¼ in [6 mm] thickness. It's super important to roll out the clay as evenly as possible. Once a large clay slab has been formed, use the X-Acto knife to cut two 2 by 3 in [5 by 7.5 cm] rectangles (for the front and back of the juice box), one 1 by 2 in [2.5 by 5 cm] rectangle for the bottom (base) of the juice box, one 1½ by 2 in [4 by 5 cm] rectangle for the top, two 1 by 3 in [2.5 by 7.5 cm] rectangles (for the sides), two 1½ by 1 by 1 in [4 by 2.5 by 2.5 cm] triangles for the decorative flaps and one ½ by 2 in [13 mm by 5 cm] rectangle—this will be the photo-holding piece.

NIFTY GIFTY

**2** Take one of the 2 by 3 in [5 by 7.5 cm] rectangles and use the X-Acto knife to score x's along one of the short sides (see page 34). This will be the front of the juice box.

Add some slip to the scored edges and attach the two rectangles to each other.

**3** Do the same to the rest of the rectangles to build up the walls of the juice box. Remember to score and slip all the edges. Add coils of clay to areas that might need some extra reinforcement.

cont'd →

**4** Once all of the rectangles forming the body of the juice box are joined, attach the ½ by 2 in [13 mm by 5 cm] rectangle to the center of the top of the box and attach the triangles (inverted) to the top of the sides of the box. As you join all of the clay pieces together, use the rounded sculpting tool to smooth out the clay where you've attached each of the walls. Once all the pieces of the box are in place, take a bit of extra time smoothing everything out with a dampened clay sponge. This helps remove imperfections like extra scratches or fingerprints.

**5** Grab the clay blade and press gently into the top of the juice box in the middle of the ½ by 2 in [13 mm by 5 cm] rectangle. This is where the picture will go, so make sure that this slit has enough depth to prop up your photo, but be careful to not pierce the clay!

**6** Grab the bendy straw (preferably one that is upcycled from an actual juice box), and carefully poke the straw through the top right corner of the juice box. Roll a small clay coil and wrap it around the straw where it meets the clay. With the rounded sculpting tool, blend this coil in to reinforce the straw. Let the juice box dry for 24 to 48 hours (follow the instructions on the package of the air-dry clay).

Once it's completely dry, it's time to paint! When the paint is completely dry, brush the juice box with a light coat of acrylic varnish to make your project more durable.

> This picture holder is fairly simple to make, but your creativity can truly run wild when it comes to the decoration of this craft. I decided to paint mine to resemble the juice box emoji, so I used green and white and then red for the apple in the center. But there are, like, a billion juice boxes to draw inspiration from. If your bestie prefers orange juice, draw an orange juice label or grape, or peach, or pineapple, or kiwi . . . you get the idea.

**THE ART OF**

# Scoring and Slipping

Clay is an incredible and easy-to-use medium: From trinket dishes to picture frames, jewelry, and more, there's no limit to the fun and unique items you can make. But in order to really master the art of using clay, you need to know two simple but key techniques—scoring and slipping—that are used to join two pieces of clay together securely.

- **Scoring:** The process of making small cuts or scratches on the edges of the pieces of clay that you want to join together. This creates a surface that the clay pieces can easily adhere to. To score, use the following tools:
    - → X-Acto knife
    - → Fettling knife
    - → Needle tool
    - → Serrated rib tool

- **Slipping:** The process of applying slip (water and clay mixture paste) to the scored areas, acting as a sort of "glue." To make a slip, add 2 parts clay and 1 part water to a resealable plastic container or glass jar and mix until you have a gravy-like consistency. To slip, use the following tools:
    - → Small or medium paintbrush
    - → Flat-edge clay tool

Together these techniques help ensure that your clay creation is smooth and durable. It also avoids cracking during the drying process.

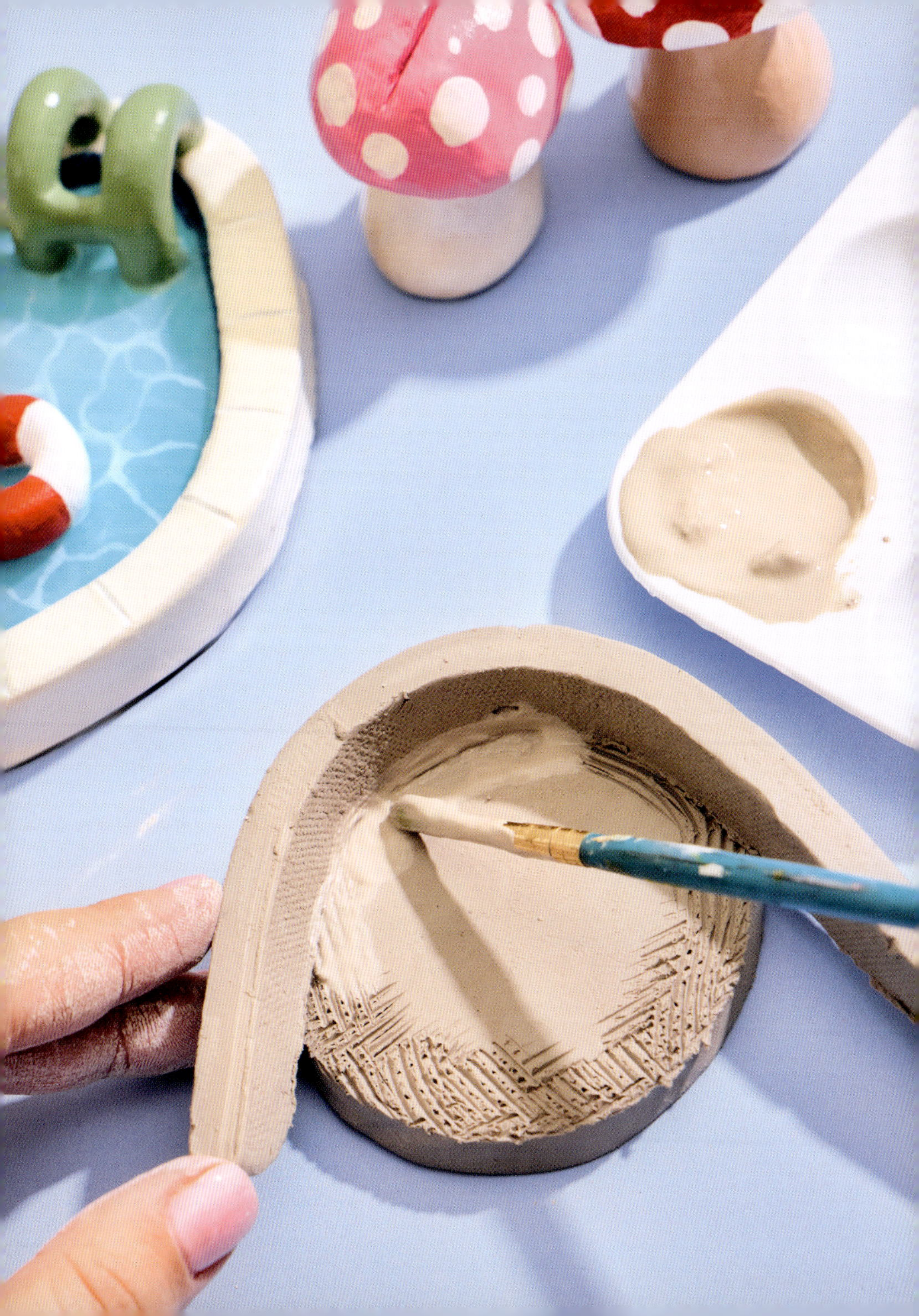

# Mini Trinket Shelf

**CRAFTING TIME: 45-55 MINUTES**

This gift is perfect for that friend who has an army of collectibles, from jewelry to Sonny Angels, and has run out of space to display them all.

I personally love having places to put more trinkets. Some would call me a hoarder; I would say I'm just a gatherer of cute things! This specific trinket holder is great for displaying exactly one very special trinket. The golden trinket, if you will. This cute lil trinket shelf might not be that big—but that just gives you an excuse to make a lot of them. 😉

I went for a minimalist look: I covered my trinket shelf in white acrylic paint and then added a blue flower with a white center and a simple blue-and-white pattern around the edge of the shelf. For a more maximalist look, paint the shelf a bright red and add white flowers with dark green stems to the inside and outside of the walls in a scattered fashion until the entire shelf is covered in a flower pattern. Or, if you're going for a more feminine look, paint the shelf a light pink and paint a white bow on the inside of the shelf. Then on the outside walls, paint a line of white hearts going all the way around the outer dome.

**SUPPLIES**

Canvas mat (optional)

Plastic or acrylic rolling pin

1 lb [455 g] air-dry clay

X-Acto knife

Scoring and slipping tools of your choice (see page 34)

Rounded sculpting tool

Needle tool

Clay sponge

Paintbrushes

Acrylic paint

Acrylic varnish

On Being Nice

1. On a canvas mat or a clean and flat surface, use the rolling pin to roll the clay out to a ½ in [13 mm] thickness. Remember to take your time rolling the clay out to ensure an even thickness throughout. Using an X-Acto knife, cut out a 3 by 3 in [7.5 by 7.5 cm] squircle, a.k.a. a rectangle with a semicircle top. This will be the base or back of the trinket shelf. Cut out two clay ribbons. One should be about 10 by 1 in [25 by 2.5 cm] for the perimeter minus the base of the squircle. The other ribbon should be about 3 by 1 in [7.5 by 2.5 cm]. These two ribbons will make up the walls of the trinket shelf.

2. Score and slip along the top edges of the squircle and along the length of the ribbons that will be attached to the base (see page 34). Attach the ribbons to the base and blend them together with your fingers or the rounded sculpting tool. Reinforce the corners by rolling out small coils of clay, placing them in the corners, and blending those in.

**3** Using your needle tool, poke out a hole ½ in [13 mm] in diameter at the top of the base.

**4** Smooth out any imperfections with a dampened clay sponge. Let the shelf dry for 24 to 48 hours (follow the instructions on the package of air-dry clay).

Once the clay is fully dry, it's ready to be painted! When the paint is dry, brush the shelf with a light coat of varnish to make your project more durable.

MINI TRINKET SHELF

# Strawberry Trinket Dish

**CRAFTING TIME: 30–45 MINUTES**

Strawberries are the quintessential summer fruit, and they're just aesthetically pleasing. Take Strawberry Shortcake for example: She is an icon!

This fruit-themed dish is simple to make and a perfect summer craft that'll add a pop of color in your room or your bestie's room. Not to mention it'll be an ideal place to stash little trinkets, rings, earrings, bracelets, or necklaces. Storing jewelry has never looked this adorable.

Don't be alarmed by the apparent difficulty for this craft. It's still simple but has complex steps. I'll guide you every step of the way so your strawberry trinket dish comes out looking absolutely adorable!

**SUPPLIES**

Canvas mat (optional)

Plastic or acrylic rolling pin

1 lb [455 g] air-dry clay

2 pieces of paper (5 by 6 in [13 by 15 cm] and 2 by 5 in [5 by 13 cm])

Permanent marker

Scissors

Fettling knife

Loop tool

Rounded sculpting tool

Clay sponge

Scoring and slipping tools of your choice (see page 34)

Paintbrushes (like a small tapered brush, medium flat-head brush, large round brush)

Acrylic paint (red, green, and yellow)

Acrylic varnish

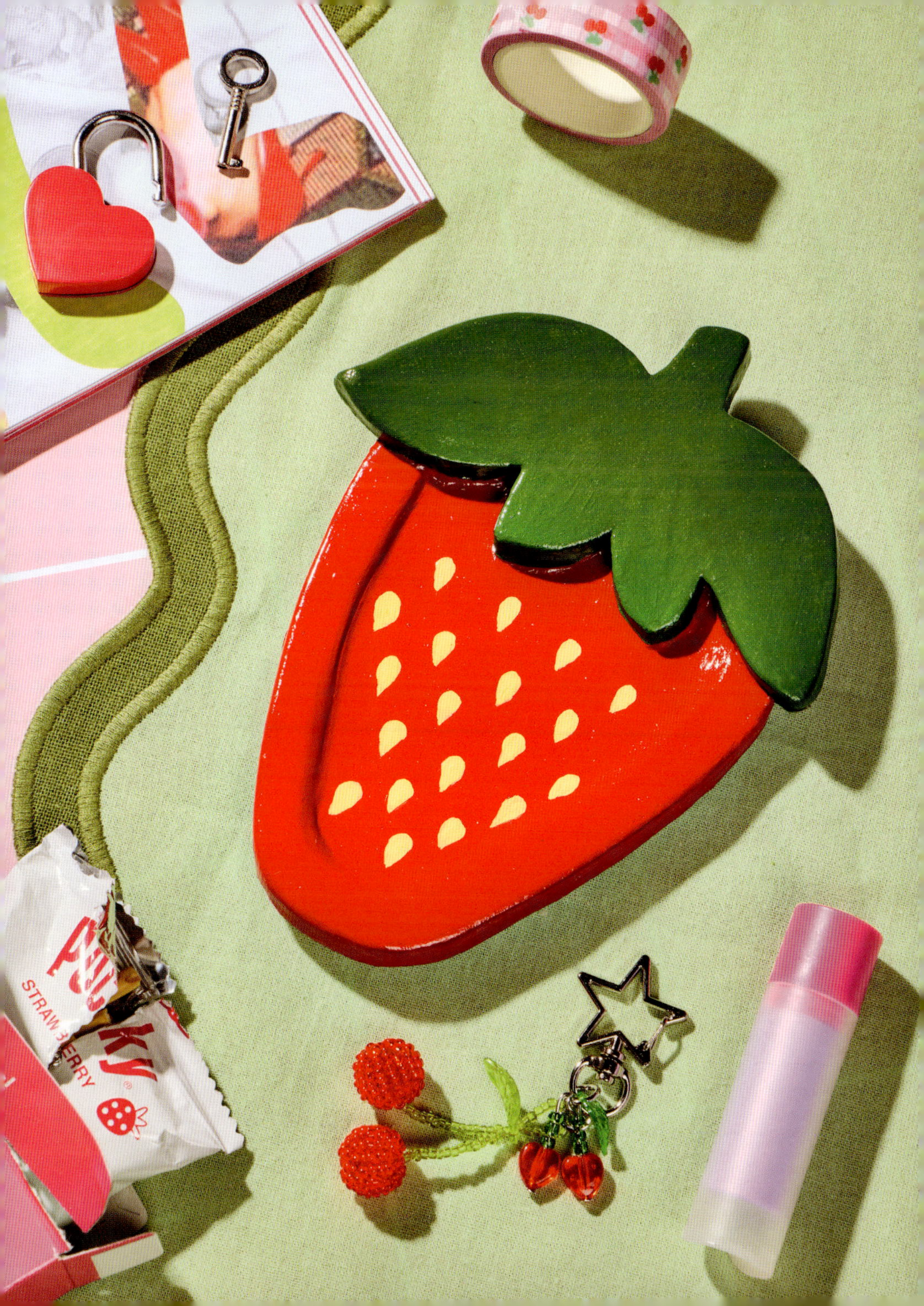

**1** On a canvas mat or a clean and flat surface, use the rolling pin to roll the clay out to a ½ in [13 mm] thickness. Print or draw an outline of a strawberry shape (body) on the piece of paper that is 5 by 6 in [13 by 15 cm] and draw the shape of the strawberries leaves (top) on the piece of paper that is 2 by 5 in [5 by 13 cm]. Using scissors, cut out the shapes. Place the shapes on top of the clay slab and trace around them, using the fettling knife to cut them out of the slab.

**2** Set aside the top and grab the body piece. Using the loop tool, start carving out the dish in the middle of the clay, about ¼ in [6 mm] in depth, leaving ½ in [13 mm] around the perimeter. Be careful to not carve too far down, because it'll create a hole in your dish, and you don't want that! Once the dish is roughly carved out, use your fingers or the rounded sculpting tool to press down and smooth out any bumps and imperfections. Use a dampened clay sponge for any final smoothing.

NIFTY GIFTY

**3** Lay the top piece on top of the body of the strawberry so the stem and a part of the leaves are slightly hanging off. Lift the leaves back off and score and slip the parts that are touching (see page 34), then blend them into each other. Be extra careful to not break off the parts that are not attached to the strawberry body (see below).

**4** Smooth out any bumps and imperfections with the dampened clay sponge. Once the strawberry trinket dish is nice and smooth and looks the way you like, set it somewhere safe to dry for 24 to 48 hours (follow the instructions on the package of air-dry clay).

Once it's fully dry, it's ready to be painted! Use a bright red to cover the body of the strawberry and a vivid green for the leaves. Add some light-yellow specks for the seeds. Once the paint has dried, brush the dish with a light coat of varnish to make your project more durable.

STRAWBERRY TRINKET DISH

# Mini Pool-Shaped Trinket Dish

**CRAFTING TIME: 1 HOUR**

**SUPPLIES**

Whew! It's time to cool down from making all these crafts. What better way to end the day than in the pool lounging on a floatie?

This craft really makes me wish I had a pool in my backyard, and this gift is perfect for that friend who likes collecting tiny versions of big things and having them on display as decor in their home/space. If someone made this lil trinket dish for me, I think I would fill an entire pool with my happy tears because it's so adorable, and I would be grateful that someone spent so much time and dedication making me such a cool and one-of-a-kind gift.

**Canvas mat (optional)**

**Plastic or acrylic rolling pin**

**1 lb [455 g] air-dry clay**

**Fettling knife**

**Scoring and slipping tools (see page 34), preferably a serrated rib tool**

**Rounded sculpting tool**

**Clay sponge**

**Needle tool**

**Paintbrushes**

**Acrylic paint (blue, beige, and green)**

**Acrylic varnish**

**UV resin and UV nail lamp (optional; see note)**

NIFTY GIFTY

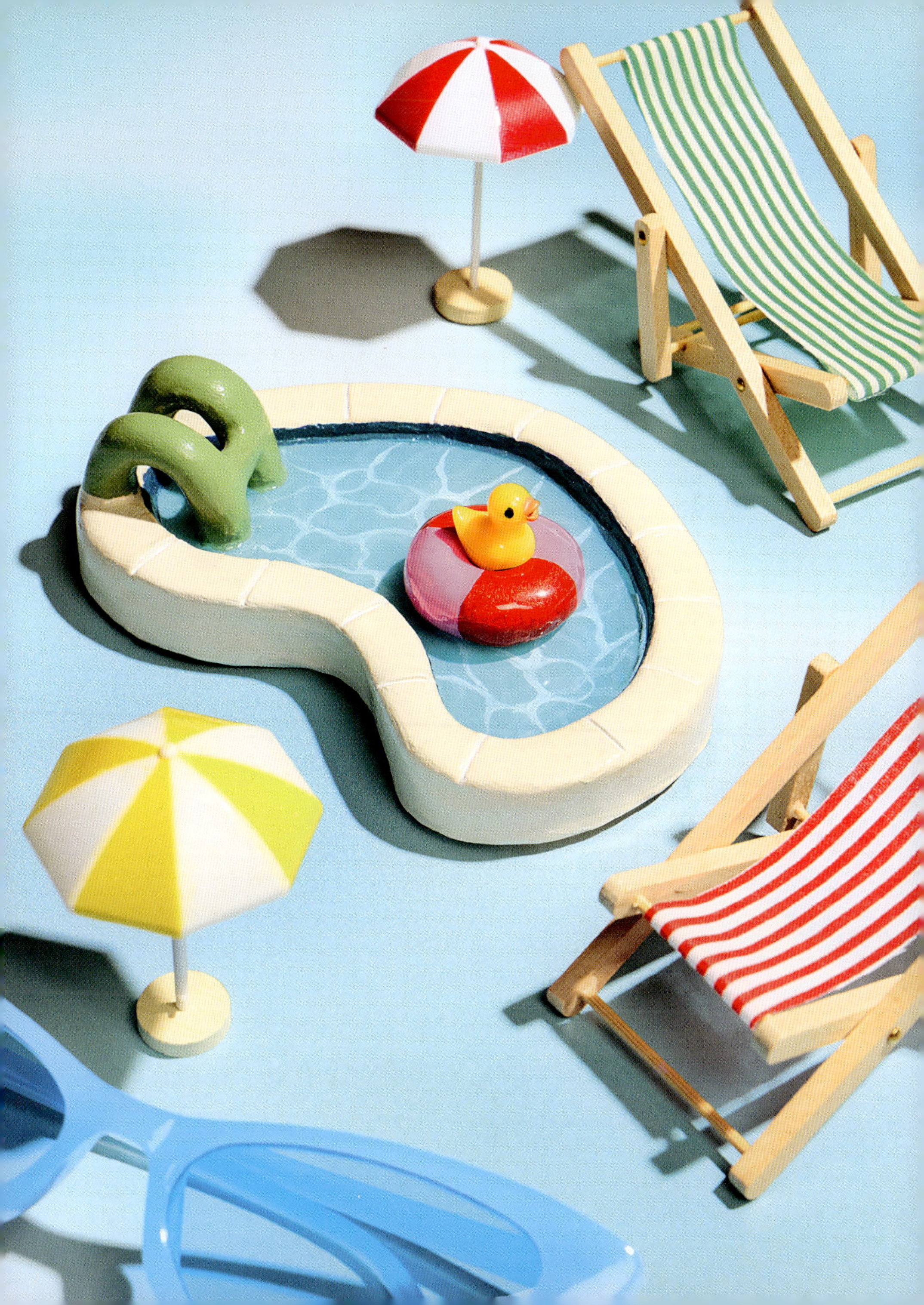

1. On a canvas mat or a clean and flat surface, use the rolling pin to roll half of the clay out to a ½ in [13 mm] thickness. Using the fettling knife, cut out a kidney bean shape that is roughly 5 by 3 in [13 by 7.5 cm].

2. With the rolling pin, roll out the remaining half of the clay into a slab about ½ in [13 mm] thick. This slab needs to be more long than wide. Cut out a clay ribbon that is ¾ in [2 cm] wide and long enough to go around the whole perimeter of the kidney shape. This will be the walls of the pool.

3. Score and slip along the bottom side of the long ribbon and on the top perimeter of the kidney bean shape (see page 34).

cont'd →

NIFTY GIFTY           46

MINI POOL-SHAPED TRINKET DISH

4. Attach the scored sides to each other and blend them together using your fingers or the rounded sculpting tool to smooth out any gaps or imperfections in the clay. It should look like a kidney bean trinket dish at this point.

5. With the remaining clay, roll out two 1½ in [4 cm] coils that are ⅓ in [8.5 mm] thick. These will be used to make a pool ladder. Score and slip both ends of the first coil and attach one end to the "edge" of the pool and the other end to inside of the pool, creating a candy cane shape. Repeat with the other coil, placing it next to the first coil so they're about ½ in [13 mm] apart. Roll out a much smaller and thinner coil that is ¼ in [6 mm] long and attach it to the inside of the larger coils to create the step. Smooth out the whole dish with a dampened clay sponge.

**6** Using the needle tool, create slight line indentations around the edge of the pool to make it look like a brick pattern. Let the dish dry for 24 to 48 hours (follow the instructions on the package of air-dry clay).

When the clay is dry, it's ready to be painted. I used blue for the inside of the pool to mimic water, beige or khaki for the outside "brick," and green for the pool ladder. Once the paint is dry, brush the pool with a light coat of varnish to make your project more durable.

> If you'd like a more realistic water look, pour in about 1/8 in [3 mm] of UV resin (or just enough to fill the inside of the pool) and cure the resin for 5 minutes under a UV nail lamp. It'll look like a small layer of water!

MINI POOL-SHAPED TRINKET DISH

**BONUS: MINI CLAY FLOATIE**

1. Roll out a thick clay coil and attach the ends to itself to create a donut shape.

2. Use your fingers or clay tool of choice to merge and smooth out both ends of the coil until the floatie is seamless. Make sure that the size will fit in your mini pool.

NIFTY GIFTY

**3** Let the clay dry and then paint it in a classic red and white pattern or any colors you choose.

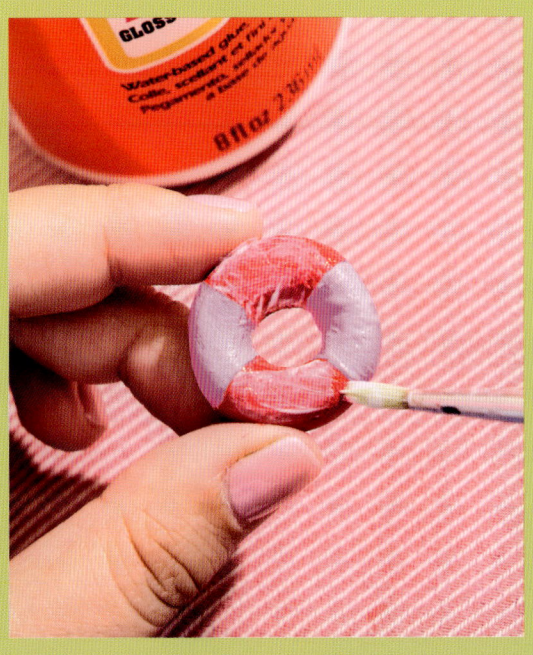

**4** Once the paint is dry, brush the floatie with a light coat of varnish. Allow it to dry completely before placing it inside of the mini pool trinket dish.

MINI POOL-SHAPED TRINKET DISH

# Bejeweled Lighter

CRAFTING TIME: 25-35 MINUTES

Yass! For those of you who are new to the word *yassified*, it means to give someone, or something, a makeover. I could have called this craft a lighter makeover, but where's the fun in that, you know? Lighters are such common accessories they often get overlooked, but they too can be unique objects.

This gift is perfect for that person in your life who enjoys lighting candles or for the friend who always likes to have a lighter on hand for social gatherings. Pulling out a decorated lighter is a surefire conversation starter. It can give people insight into your personality or just earn you some cool points.

This simple craft also makes for an amazing group activity! Gathering your girls for a wine and yassified lighter night is so iconic.

**SUPPLIES**

**Nail file or sandpaper**

**Classic BIC lighter**

**Sparkly decorations of choice (like rhinestones, stickers, or beads)**

**Strong silicone glue (like E6000)**

**Toothpicks**

**Bedazzling pen or tweezers (optional)**

*If you want your decorated lighter to be even more unique, try incorporating other decorative elements like 3D stickers, acrylic nail charms, mini fuzzy pom poms, and even fake flowers.*

NIFTY GIFTY

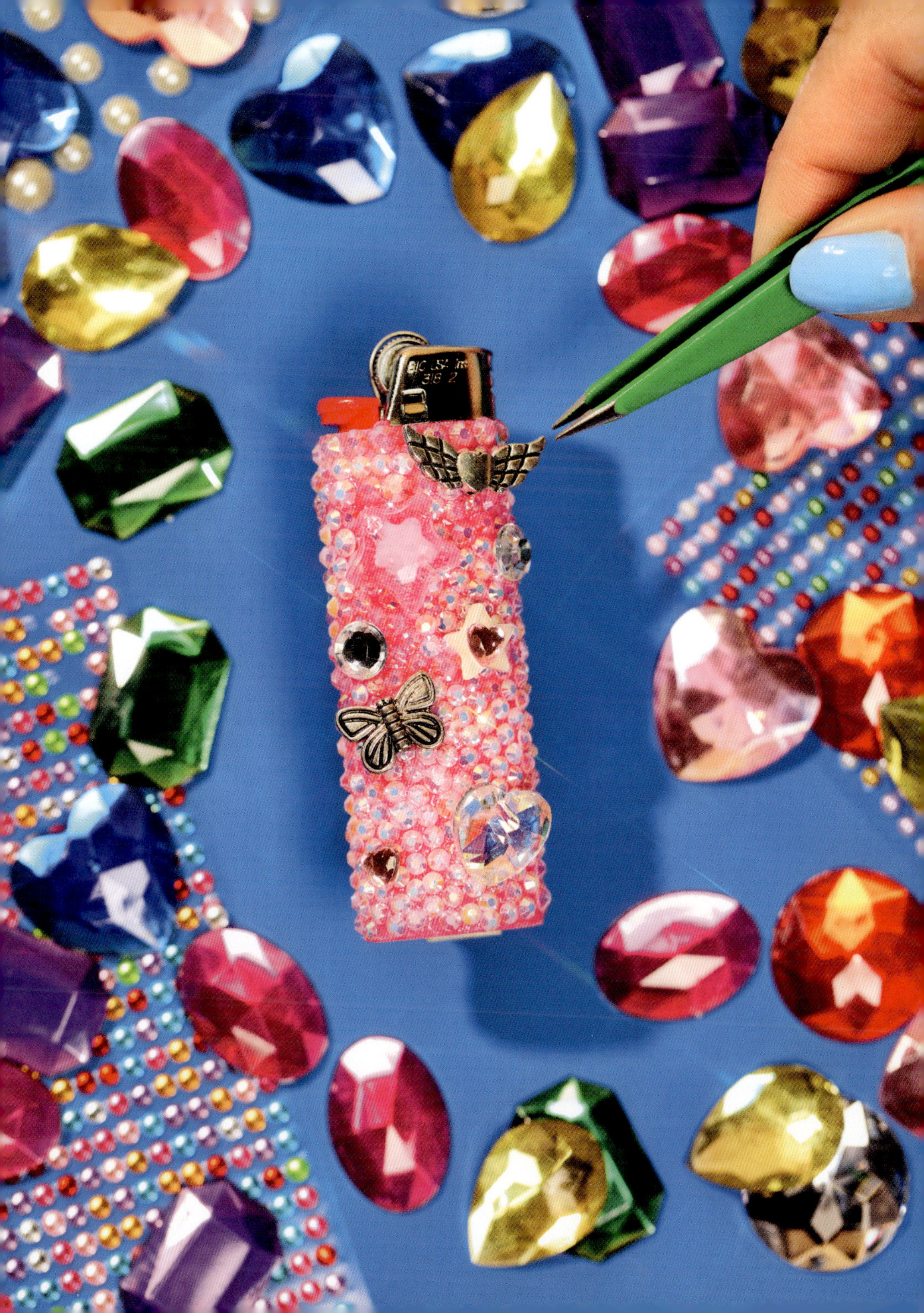

1. Use a nail file or sandpaper to scratch up the surface of the lighter. Getting rid of the top coating on the plastic makes it easier for the glue and beads to stay on.

2. Gather all the decorations you would like to use.

**3** Squeeze a little silicone glue onto a surface. This will make it easier to apply glue as you bedazzle and decorate. Use a toothpick to scoop up a small amount of the glue and start spreading it out on a section of the lighter.

**4** If you have a bedazzling pen or tweezers, use that to carefully pick up each rhinestone and set them where you spread the glue. If you do not have a bedazzling pen, dipping the tip of a toothpick into silicone glue to create a silicone ball tip will work just as well! As you decorate, go section by section, allowing each section to dry a bit before moving on to the next. Repeat until the lighter is fully decorated on all sides—yassified!

BEJEWELED LIGHTER

**HOW TO**

# Host a Crafting Night

Hosting a crafting night is a fun, interactive activity to elevate any dinner party or gathering amongst friends. Here are some tips to get you started:

- Start off by deciding what craft would be ideal in a group setting. I suggest keeping it simple to be mindful about new crafters!

- Set the vibes for the craft night and decorate the crafting space accordingly. I suggest setting down a tablecloth or covering for your crafting surface since things might get messy (in a fun, creative way). Once this is done, set up the crafting tables with all the supplies the guests will need. You can even break out the fine china to hold various craft supplies to really elevate the vibes.

- Once your supplies are set, place snacks and drinks nearby, because what's a crafting party without some good snacks? Prepping a good craft table will set you up for a smooth and relaxing evening full of yapping and crafting with your favorite people!

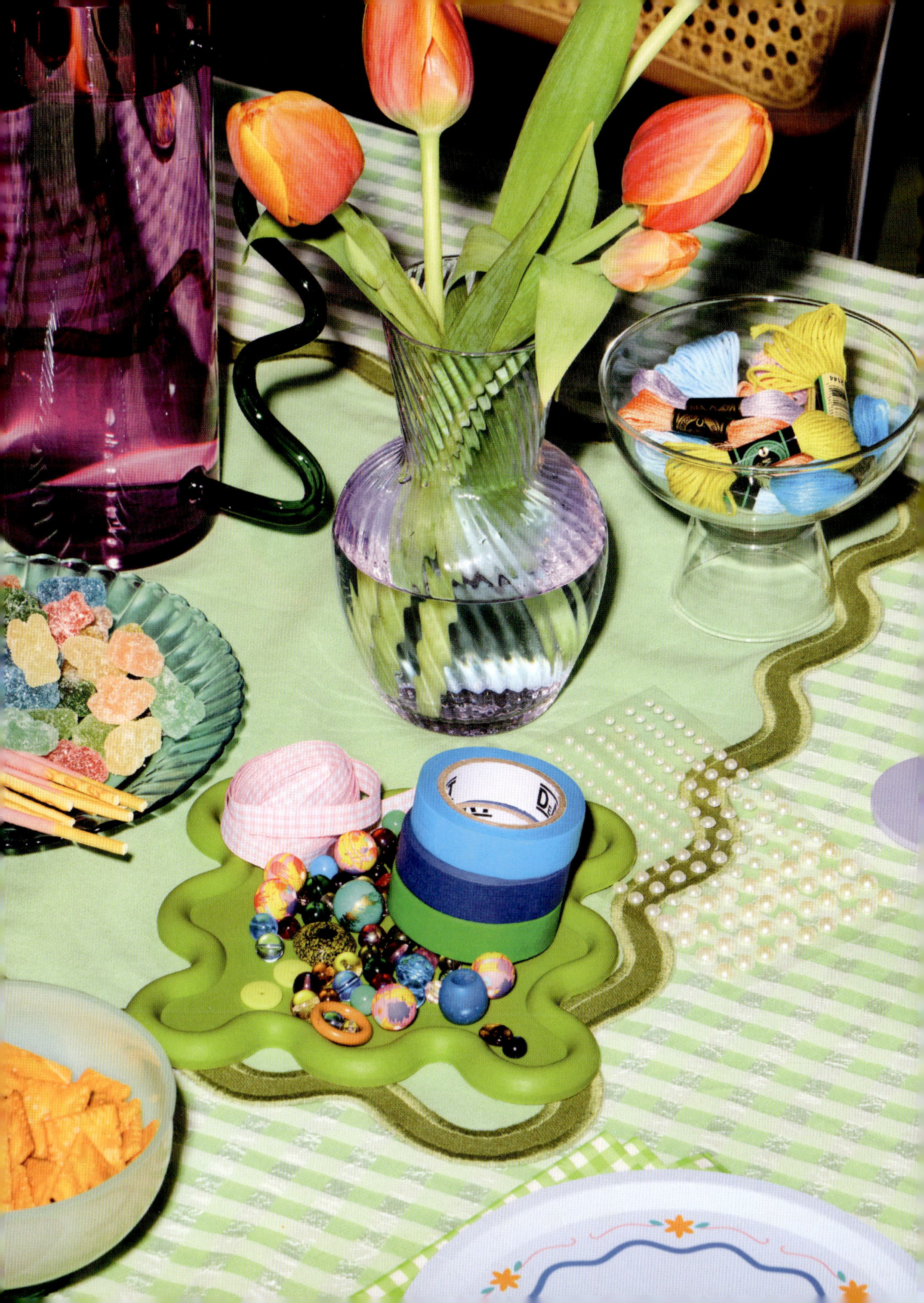

# Mint Tin Wallet

CRAFTING TIME: 30-45 MINUTES

A mint tin wallet is perfect for your friend who still wears wired earbuds, Vans, and winged eyeliner—think coquettish aesthetics and early Tumblr/Lana Del Rey vibes.

The beauty of this craft is that it can be decorated and embellished with supplies already found in your craft bin: stickers, ribbons, scrapbook paper, and more.

And this gift doesn't have to only be a wallet. Let's say your friend is a little bit messy, but you love them anyway. You'll make their life so much easier with this small-but-mighty carrying case: Instead of digging through a giant bag looking for a hair tie, lip balm, or their tangled-up earbuds, they can easily store all those necessities in this cute tin.

> The initial idea for this mint tin wallet was to give it a coquette vibe, but that can easily be changed depending on the decorative elements added to the wallet. For example, adding seashells and more coastal colors on the inside of the tin will change the whole vibe, making it fit into a more coastal aesthetic. Or adding crystals, crescent moon and sun stickers, and star charms can give it a mystical, witchy vibe.

## SUPPLIES

Mint tin

Pencil

**Different kinds of paper of choice (like newspaper, scrapbook paper, card stock, etc.)**

**Scissors**

**Small mirror (This can be an upcycled or repurposed mirror. Check any old makeup compacts—you may be able to pop out the mirror from one of those.)**

**Strong silicone glue (like E6000)**

**Decorations of choice (like stickers, rhinestones, and ribbons)**

je t'aime

1. Trace the bottom and top of the mint tin onto scrapbook paper of your choice. Cut these pieces out and glue them to the inside of the mint tin.

2. Choose the best place for the mirror. I like to put it on the inside of the lid so the mint tin mimics a makeup compact. Squeeze a thin layer of glue onto the back of the mirror and press it into place.

**3** Once the glue is dry, the mint tin is ready to be decorated. Add sparkly stickers all over the outside of the tin. Glue rhinestones along the edges of the mirror to give it a fabulous frame. Add a small ribbon bow at the top of the mirror.

**4** After decorating your tin, fill it with your bestie's favorite essentials: lip tint, bobby pins, hair ties, glasses wipes, or a mini picture of you two together.

# Funky Bookmarks

CRAFTING TIME: 10 MINUTES FOR EACH

**SUPPLIES**

I know what you're thinking: A little piece of paper can't possibly be a gift. Well, I would say yes, you're right, but what about a *decorated* little piece of paper, hmm?

Picture this: You've got all the gifts for your best friend ready to go but you wish you had just one more thing to tie everything together. You don't want to buy them a random card so instead you get the brilliant idea to make them something unique, heartfelt, and cool. Making them a handy lil bookmark is the perfect solution, and your friend will love the fact that you made them something one-of-a-kind and memorable. You can even write a birthday message on the back of the bookmark, so it's a double win.

I went a little over the top with this one and provided you with three different designs.

**Mixed media paper**

**Scissors**

**Ruler**

**Masking tape**

**Markers**

**Spray fixative (optional)**

**Yarn or twine**

**Hole punch**

**Lipstick (for Kisses design)**

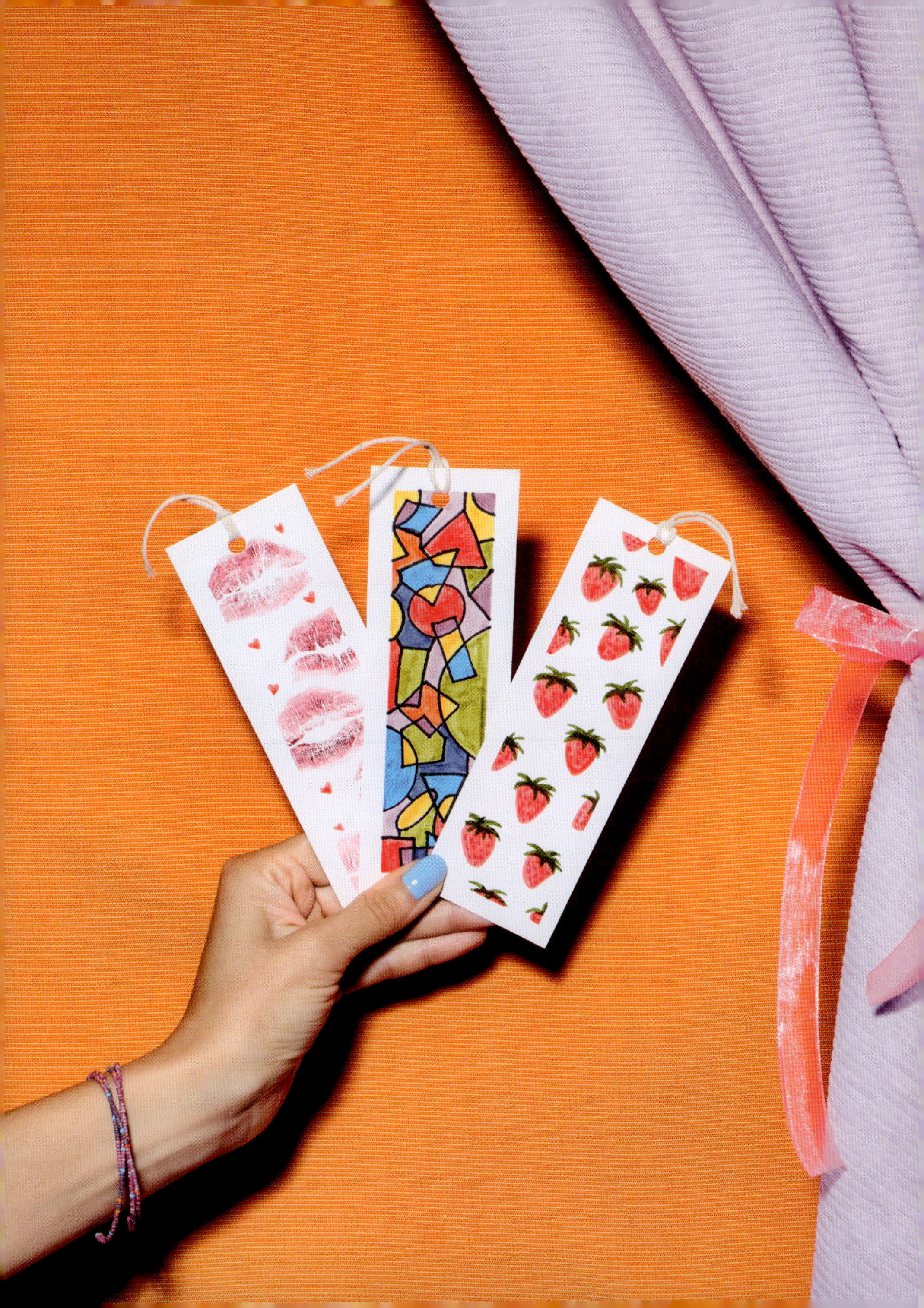

1. Cut out a 6 by 2 in [15 by 5 cm] piece of the mixed media paper. Using masking tape, tape the paper to your work surface, covering ¼ in [6 mm] all along its border.

**DESIGN 1: STRAWBERRY**

1. Grab a red marker and begin drawing triangles with rounded corners all over the paper. These are the bodies of little strawberries. Have some go off the page to make it more visually pleasing. Next, grab a light green marker and add leaves to the tops of the strawberries. As a final touch, grab a darker green marker to add dimension to the leaves and a darker red marker to add the lil seeds.

2. Peel off the masking tape very carefully. Seal the paper with spray fixative or any clear paper sealant, if desired. Cut 6 in [15 cm] of yarn or twine. Punch a hole ½ in [13 mm] from the top of the bookmark in the center. Fold the yarn in half to form a loop. Feed the loop through the hole, then feed the two ends of the yarn through the loop. Tug to secure the knot.

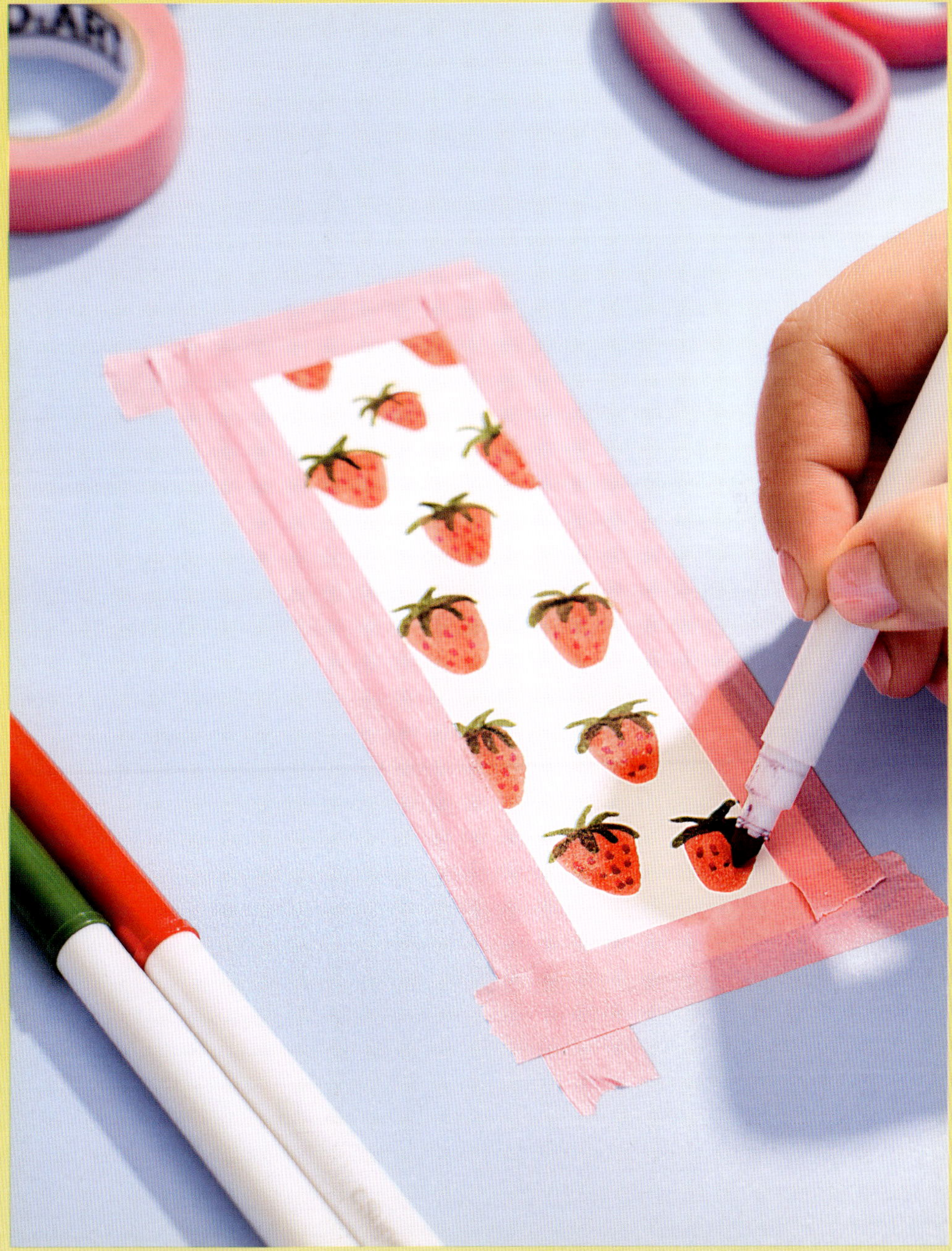

**NIFTY GIFTY**

**DESIGN 2: FUNKY STAINED GLASS**

1. With a black marker, draw randomly sized circles all over the paper. Next, add in triangles. Make sure some of the shapes start to overlap. Then start adding in more shapes like squares, rhombuses, ovals, etc. Have those shapes overlap as well.

2. Now that there is a jumble of shapes on the page, begin to fill in spaces with different colors. We've essentially created a mini coloring page. Use at least five different colored markers to fill in the spaces. Once everything is filled in, you can see the funky stained-glass pattern.

3. Carefully remove the masking tape and seal the paper with the spray fixative or any clear paper sealant, if desired. Cut 6 in [15 cm] of yarn or twine. Punch a hole ½ in [13 mm] from the top of the bookmark in the center. Fold the yarn in half to form a loop. Feed the loop through the hole, then feed the two ends of the yarn through the loop. Tug to secure the knot.

NIFTY GIFTY

**DESIGN 3: KISSES**

**1** Grab your favorite shades of lipstick and cover the whole sheet with different-colored kisses. Allow the lipstick to dry and then seal the bookmark with the spray fixative.

**2** Cut 6 in [15 cm] of yarn or twine. Punch a hole ½ in [13 mm] from the top of the bookmark in the center. Fold the yarn in half to form a loop. Feed the loop through the hole, then feed the two ends of the yarn through the loop. Tug to secure the knot.

> To make this even more personal, gift this with a book you think the giftee will love and decorate the bookmark to match the vibes of the story.

FUNKY BOOKMARKS

# Eraser Stamp

**CRAFTING TIME: 30 MINUTES**

**SUPPLIES**

Stamps! They're like stickers but more fun because they can be used over and over on a plethora of surfaces. This gift isn't just an eraser with a design carved out of it. It's also the repeating design that your giftee can make across different surfaces—the most customizable gift yet. However, if your friend loves to collect stamps then be my guest: Make them a whole army of custom stamps!

I used one to make a custom design for a friend's small business, one to sign off a letter to my bestie, and another to make a custom print for my home.

Keep in mind that the simpler your design is, the simpler it'll be to carve out. Shapes like hearts, stars, squiggle lines, and circles are more beginner friendly and are easier to carve. For example, an easy sun stamp would consist of carving a circle and then some squiggle lines branching out of it, and boom, you've got yourself a sun stamp.

**Black permanent marker**

**Erasers**

**Light color permanent marker (like a highlighter)**

**Linoleum cutter tool**

**Colorful water-based markers**

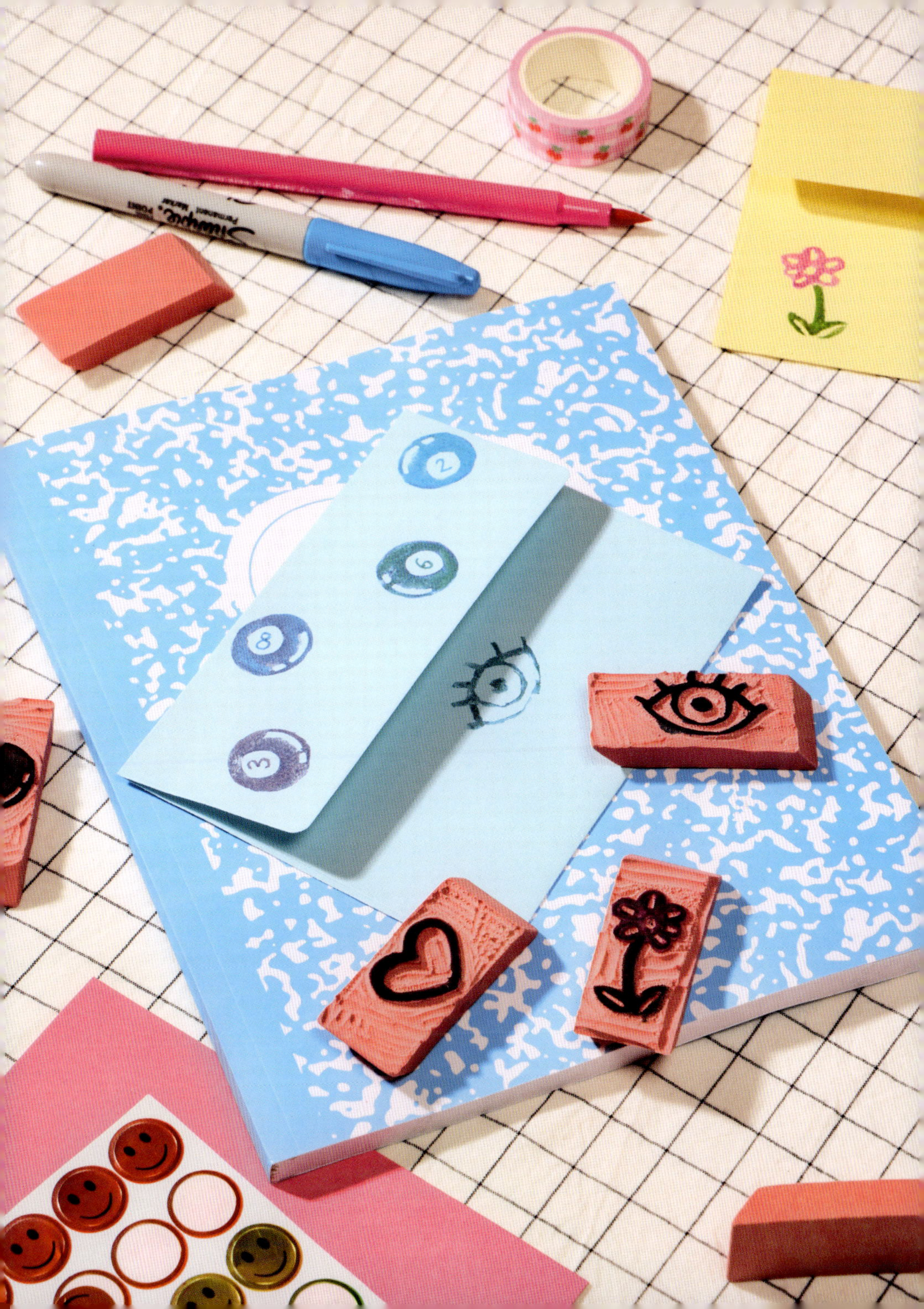

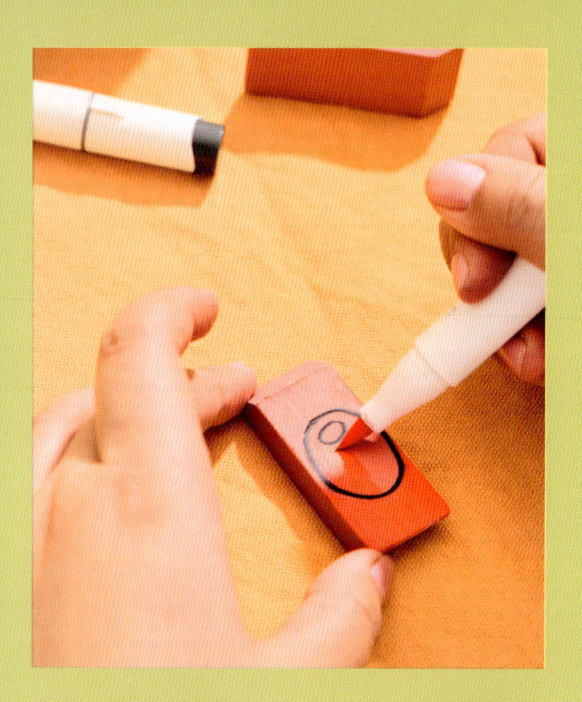

**1** Using the black permanent marker, begin drawing your stamp design on the back or smoothest side of the eraser. Once the design is finished, using the light color permanent marker, cover the entire surface of where your design is in the light color. This will help you visualize what areas need to be carved out so your eyes don't get confused.

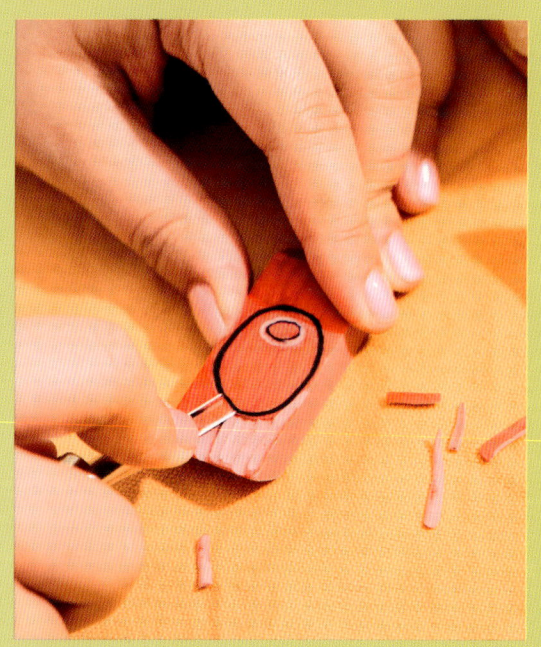

**2** Using the linoleum cutter tool, begin to carve out the areas that are not a part of your design (the light-colored areas). Once the desired areas are carved out and your stamp is finished, set it aside.

**3** Using a water-based marker of your choice, begin coloring in your stamp. Feel free to use more than one color, and make sure to really layer on the ink. The more color on the stamp, the better it'll look on the page.

**4** Press the stamp firmly onto the printing surface of your choice for 30 seconds, making sure the whole design gets transferred. Pick up the stamp gently to reveal your stamp/print.

```
      You can gift
    this stamp as is or
  use it to customize a bunch
  of different projects like:

       → Canvas totes
        → T-shirts
     → Throw pillow covers
   → Decorative kitchen towels
      → Love letter stamps
```

ERASER STAMP

# Fruit Magnets

CRAFTING TIME: 20-25 MINUTES FOR EACH

Custom magnets are such an adorable way to display memories or reminders on a fridge, a teacher's bulletin board, a locker—anything magnetic, really. These colorful, fruity, and fun crafts can make the best gift for a teacher or a housewarming gift! There are three different magnets to choose from, so feel free to make your favorite or make them all! Or if you're like me and only have three friends, make one for each. 😅

## SUPPLIES

Canvas mat (optional)

Plastic or acrylic rolling pin

½ lb [230 g] air-dry clay

Clay blade

Scoring and slipping tools of your choice (see page 34)

Rounded sculpting tool

Fine-tip paintbrush

Acrylic paints

Gloss or sealant of choice

Strong silicone glue (like E6000)

Small rounded magnets

Fettling knife (for Strawberry design)

2 mm dotting tool (for Strawberry design)

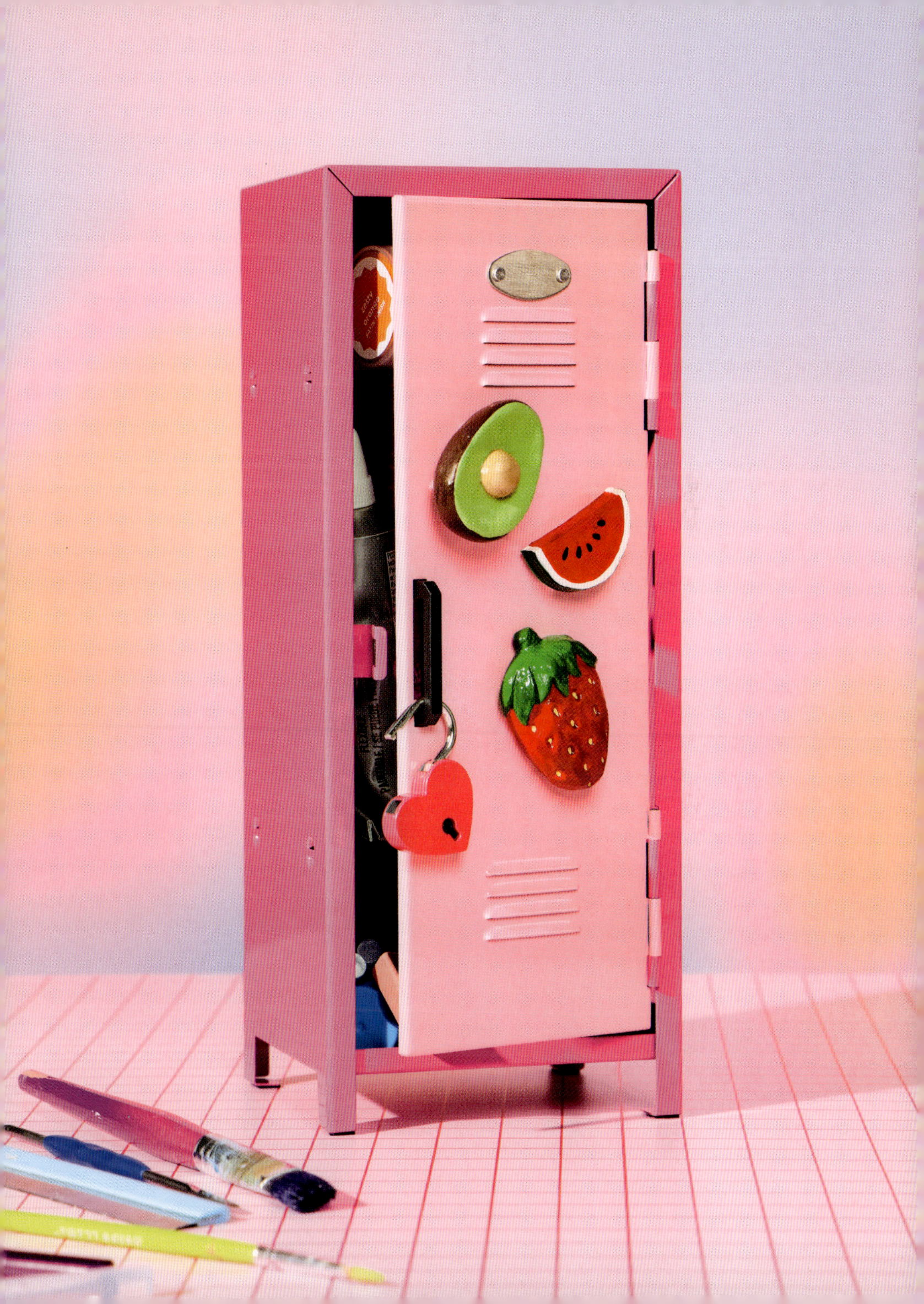

**DESIGN 1: AVOCADO**

1. On a canvas mat or a clean and flat surface, roll a piece of clay into a ball about 1 in [2.5 cm] in diameter. Press the ball against a flat surface with your fingers and begin tapping it to form a half-oval shape where one side tapers in a bit more.

2. Grab another small chunk of clay and roll it into a ball that is about ½ in [13 mm] in diameter. Using the clay blade, slice the ball in half. Score the flat side of the avocado pit and the center of the avocado (see page 34). Add some slip and attach the pit to the avocado, using a rounded sculpting tool to blend the pieces.

3. Let the avocado dry for 24 to 48 hours. Once the clay is fully dry, paint the avocado and pit. Once the paint is dry, brush the avocado with a light coat of gloss to make your project more durable. Using silicone glue, attach a magnet to the back of the avocado.

### DESIGN 2: WATERMELON

**1** On a canvas mat or a clean and flat surface, use the rolling pin to roll out a piece of clay into a slab of ¼ in [6 mm] thickness. Cut out a circle from the slab that is 1½ in [4 cm] in diameter. Using the clay blade, slice the circle into two even semicircles. Choose your desired circle half and reserve the other one for another project. Tap the edges of the semi-circle with your fingers to round it out slightly. Set it aside to dry for 24 to 48 hours.

**2** Once the clay is fully dry, paint a green stripe along the bottom of the semicircle, then a white line running next to it, and then fill the rest in with red paint. Using black paint, add a few seeds toward the top of the slice. Once the paint is dry, brush the watermelon with a light coat of gloss to make your project more durable. Using silicone glue, attach a magnet to the back of the watermelon.

**DESIGN 3: STRAWBERRY**

**1** On a canvas mat or a clean and flat surface, use the rolling pin to roll out a piece of clay into a slab of ¼ in [6 mm] thickness. Using a printed template or freehand, cut out the leaves. Take another piece of clay and roll it into a ball of about 1 in [2.5 cm] in diameter. Flatten the ball and form it into a rounded triangle shape.

**2** Gently score and slip the bottom side of the leaves and the top of the strawberry (see page 34). Add slip to the scored area of the strawberry and drape the leaves on top. Use a rounded sculpting tool to smooth and slightly press the leaves onto the strawberry.

**3** Use the fettling knife or any straight-sided wooden clay tool to make indentations at the pointed part of the leaves to give them more dimension.

**4** Use a 2 mm dotting tool to make small indentations around the strawberry. Set it aside to dry for 24 to 48 hours.

Once the clay is fully dry, paint the leaves green and the body of the strawberry red. Once the body dries, go back in and paint each indentation with a dot of white paint. Once the paint is dry, brush the strawberry with a light coat of gloss to make your project more durable. Using silicone glue, attach a magnet to the back of the strawberry.

# Selling your creations

People love buying unique handmade crafts, so if you enjoy DIY gift making as much as I do, there is definitely a way to make a profit from selling your gifts to others. Here are a couple quick tips to consider on your gift-selling journey:

- Finding your specific niche interests and crafts that you enjoy making is key to starting a successful handmade craft business. Crafts like trinket dishes or clay magnets are great items to try selling first because as humans, we love to collect things, so why not have fun themed items around the house to hold or display things in?

- A great place to sell your creations would be online, but never underestimate the appeal of local art or craft fairs. It's a great place to not only sell your crafts but also network with local creators and get advice from them.

- Don't be shy about promoting yourself and making crafting friends along the way! Always have your social media and website information handy so people can easily find and purchase your work.

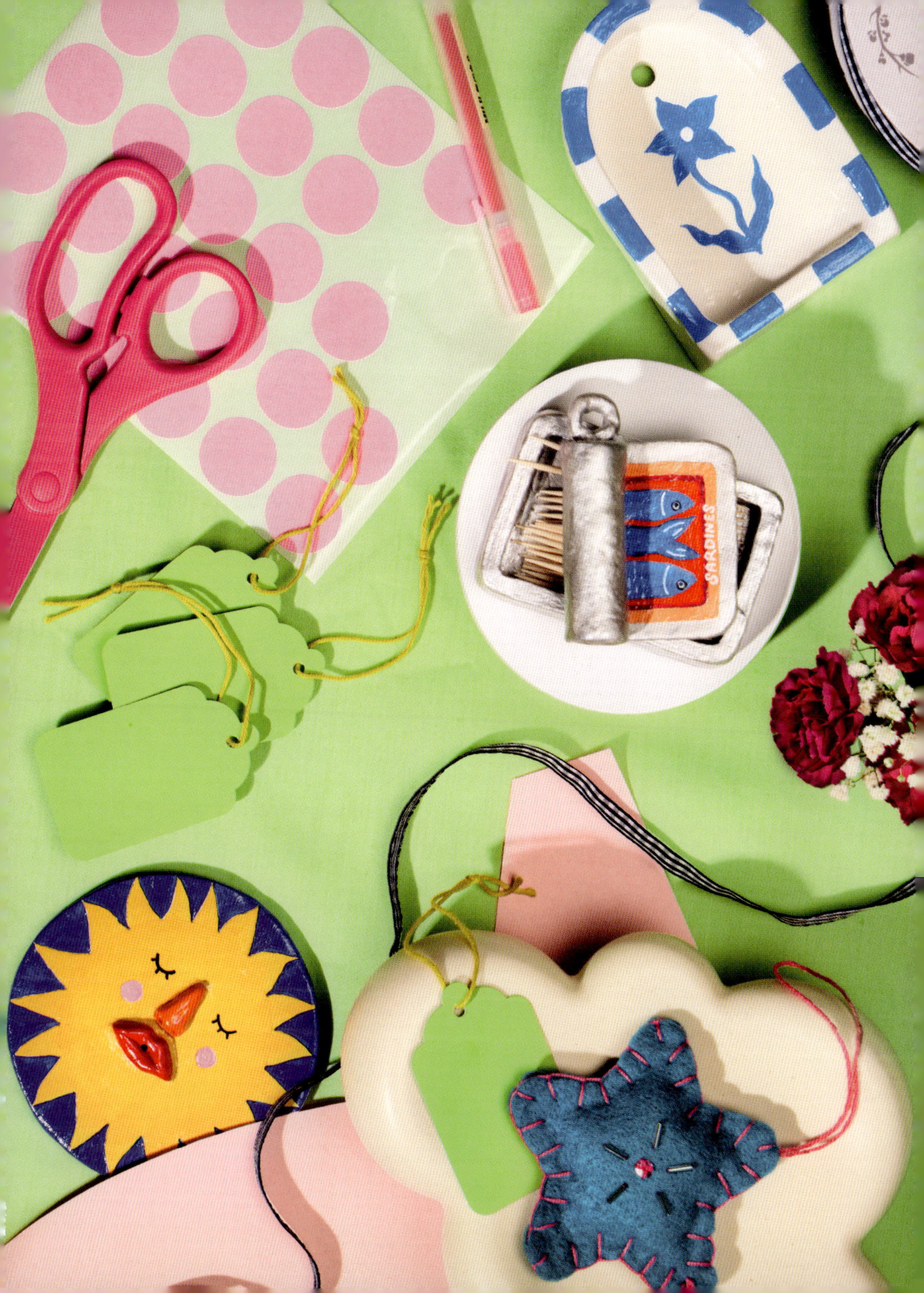
SARDINES

# Cowboy Boot Matchbox with Cowboy Hat Striker

**CRAFTING TIME: 40-55 MINUTES**

**SUPPLIES**

This one is for all of my fellow country girls! If your bestie is from the South or enjoys a lil country music, then this is the perfect gift for them.

Imagine this adorable set on their coffee table next to their flowers and Dolly Parton biography. Well, I won't keep you waitin' any longer: Let's get to craftin'!

Oh, one last thing: Make sure you let your country accent loose while making this craft. It's the only acceptable way to do it. This is a two-parter, so buckle up. Yeehaw!

Canvas mat (optional)

Plastic or acrylic rolling pin

1 lb [455 g] air-dry clay

Fettling knife

Scoring and slipping tools of your choice (see page 34)

Clay sponge

Paintbrushes

Acrylic paint

Acrylic varnish

Matches

Striker sticker

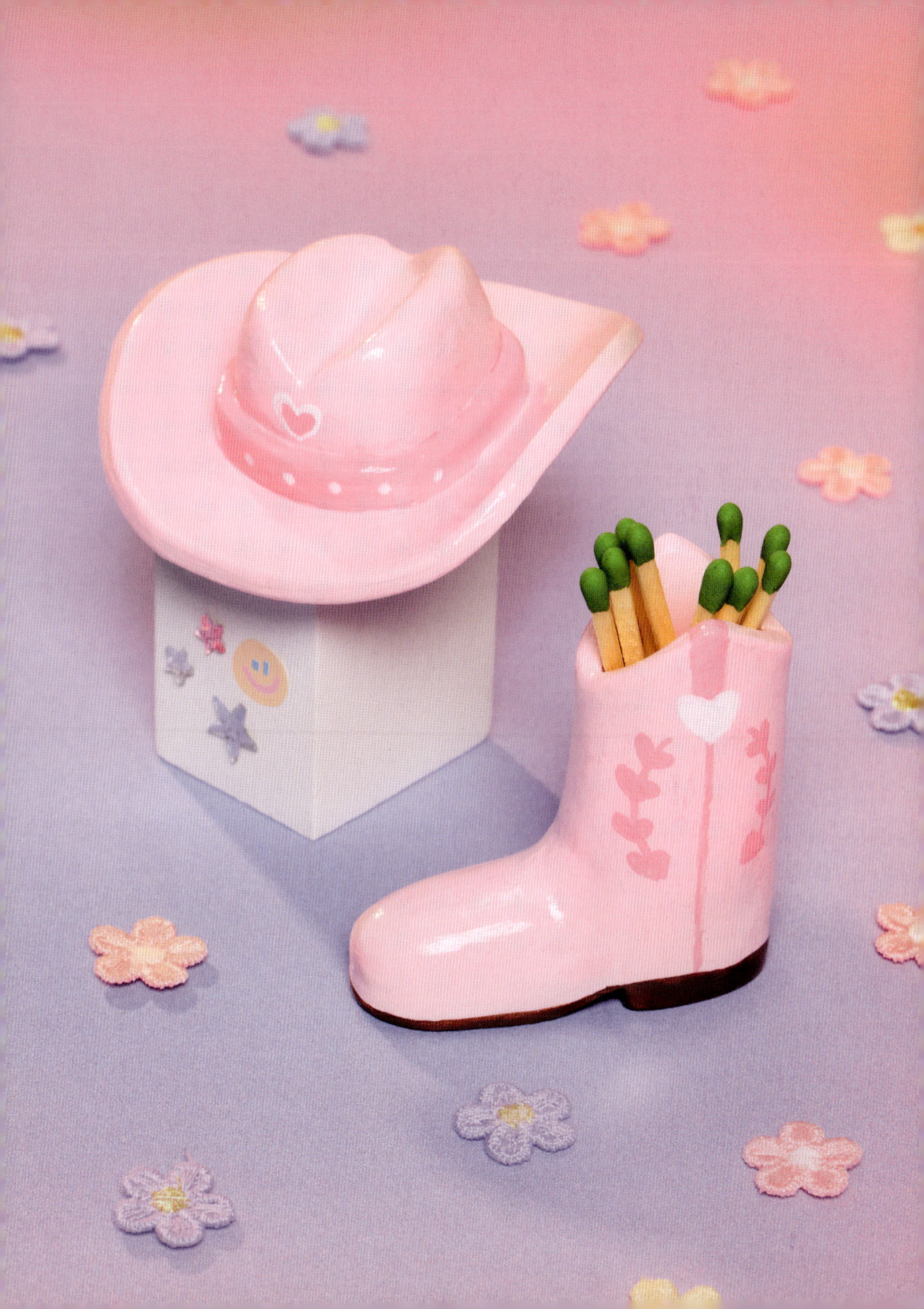

The two pieces for the neck of the boot are approximately 2 × 1½ in.

The heel length is about 1 in.

The sole is about 2½ × 1 in.

**STEPS FOR THE BOOT MATCHBOX**

1. On a canvas mat or a clean and flat surface, use the rolling pin to roll three quarters of the clay out to a ¼ in [6 mm] thickness. Use the fettling knife to cut out the four shapes pictured. These will make up the sole, heel, and neck of the boot. Stack the sole of the boot onto the heel and, with a fettling knife, blend the two clay pieces together. Score and slip (see page 34) the edges that will be attached to each other as shown.

2. Grab the two pieces that will make up the body of the boot. Slightly bend these two shapes toward each other to create a cylinder with two peaks. Blend the pieces together. Attach the cylinder to the sole of the boot, placing it above the heel.

**3** Grab a bit of clay big enough to form the toe box of the boot. Carefully sculpt and mold it to the desired shape—pointy or square.

**4** Blend and smooth everything using a dampened clay sponge. Let the clay dry for 24 to 48 hours (follow the instructions on the package of the air-dry clay).

Once the boot is completely dry, it's time to paint! You can find many cowboy boot designs online. I decided to go with a fabulous pink with a little heart—very "pink pony club." After the paint dries completely, brush the boot with a light coat of varnish to make your project more durable. After the varnish dries, fill the boot with matches.

85  COWBOY BOOT MATCHBOX WITH COWBOY HAT STRIKER

**STEPS FOR THE HAT STRIKER**

1. On a canvas mat or a clean and flat surface, use the rolling pin to roll the remaining clay out to a ¼ in [6 mm] thickness. Cut out a 2½ in [6 cm] circle using the fettling knife. Grab some of the leftover clay and roll into a ball that is about 1 to 1½ in [2.5 to 4 cm] in diameter.

2. Squish the clay ball down to create a short cylinder. This will be the top of the cowboy hat. Use the fettling knife or any straight-sided wooden clay tool to make an indentation on the top of the mini cylinder.

3. Attach the flat side of the mini cylinder to the center of the clay circle. Score and slip (see page 34) the edges that are being attached. Roll out a small clay slab and cut out a very thin strip of clay that is around ¼ in [6 mm] wide. This will be the band of the cowboy hat. Wrap the strip around the hat until both ends touch. Cut off excess if needed. Blend this strip in with your fingers or a dampened clay sponge.

NIFTY GIFTY

4 Bend the sides of the hat slightly upward—kind of like a taco—to give the clay cowboy hat some shape. Let the hat dry for 24 to 48 hours (follow the instructions on the package of the air-dry clay).

5 Once the hat is completely dry, it's time to paint! After the paint dries completely, brush the hat with a light coat of varnish to make your project more durable. Place a striker sticker on the bottom of the cowboy hat's brim.

# Sun Incense Holder

**CRAFTING TIME: 15-25 MINUTES**

Whether you or your friends enjoy lighting an incense stick for meditation, relaxation, or just for their calming scent, this sun incense holder will add a pop of color to any coffee table and bring the good vibes to any space. I've always believed that the sun has healing energies, so this little craft will definitely bring whoever you give it to some good vibrations.

**SUPPLIES**

Canvas mat (optional)

Plastic or acrylic rolling pin

½ lb [230 g] air-dry clay

Fettling knife

Needle tool or toothpick

Scoring and slipping tools of your choice (see page 34)

Incense stick

Paintbrushes

Acrylic paint (I recommend yellow, orange, red, and vivid blue)

Paint markers (optional; I recommend black and pink)

Acrylic varnish

Here's the way I paint it: Paint the center of the circle yellow, leaving ¾ in [2 cm] around the edge blank. Paint the lips a bright red and the nose orange. Using a black paint marker, add two upside-down crescents for eyes and eyelashes, and using a pink paint pen, add two small pink circles for cheeks/blush. If you don't have paint pens, use regular paint with a fine paintbrush. Paint small yellow triangles for the sun's rays around the yellow circle in the area you left blank. Fill in the rest of the blank space around the rays with vivid blue paint.

NIFTY GIFTY

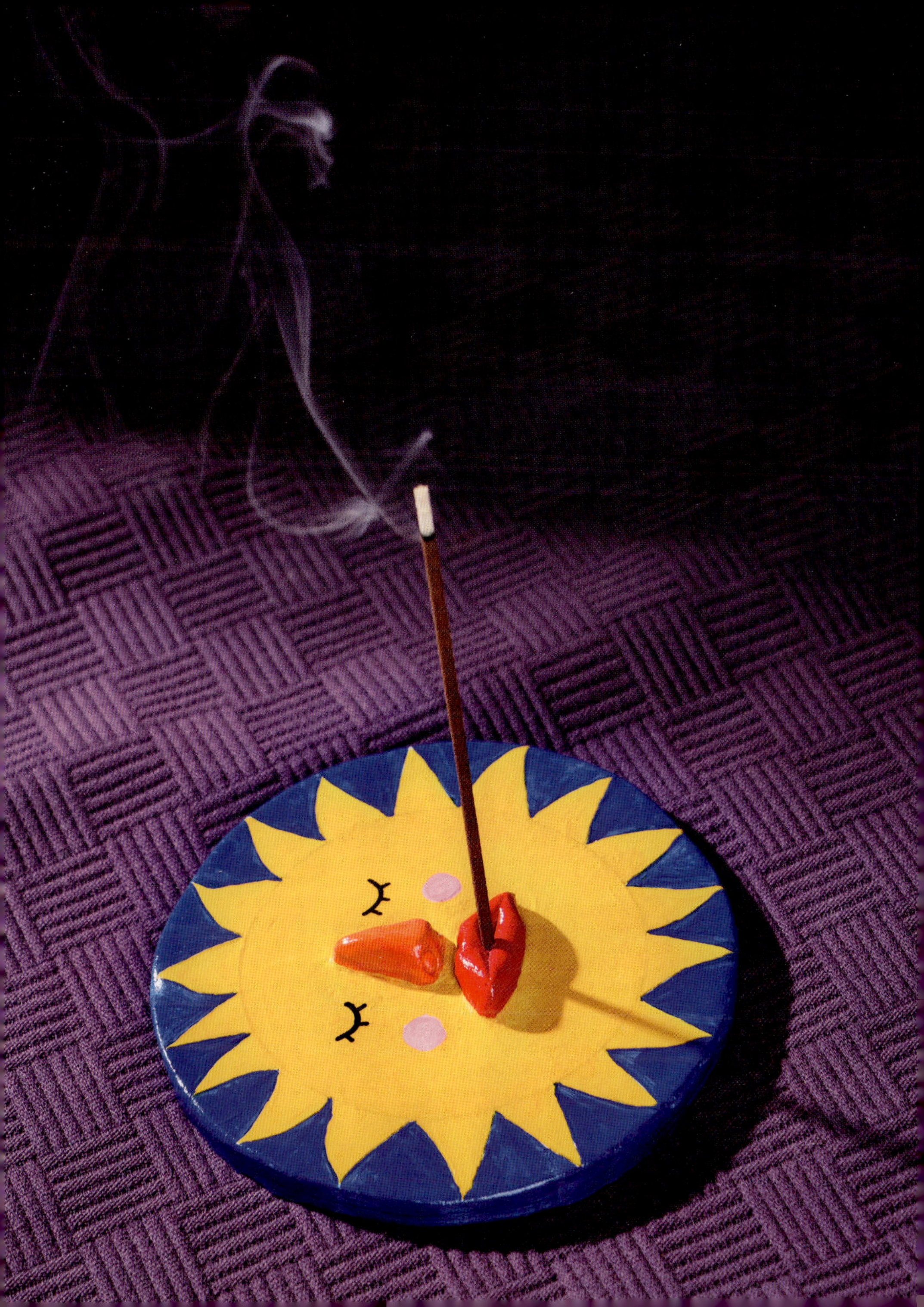

**1** On a canvas mat or a clean and flat surface, use the rolling pin to roll the clay out to a ½ in [13 mm] thickness. Use the fettling knife to cut out a circle about 4 in [10 cm] in diameter. If you have trouble cutting out perfect circles, use any circular object you have around the house and cut around it. I used a container lid!

**2** Sculpt the nose of the sun. For the nose, begin with a very small amount of clay and roll out a coil about ½ in [13 mm] long. Pinch one side of the coil to make this end taper into a dull point. It should look like a long triangle. With the needle tool or a toothpick, press in two holes at the bottom of this shape to look like nostrils. Score and slip both surfaces and attach the nose to the center of the clay circle (see page 34).

**3** For the lips, roll out two ¾ in [2 cm] long and ¼ in [6 mm] thick coils of clay. Press them together horizontally and pinch them at the ends. Using the needle tool or a toothpick, create a cupid's bow. Attach the lips about ½ in [6 mm] below the nose.

**4** Using the end of an incense stick, poke a hole in the center of the lips. Set the incense holder somewhere flat to dry for 24 to 48 hours (follow the instructions on the package of the air-dry clay).

Once the clay is fully dry, it's time to paint! I used acrylic paint on this incense holder and used paint markers for the accents. Once the paint is dry, brush the incense holder with a light coat of varnish to make your project more durable.

# Sardine Tin Toothpick Holder

CRAFTING TIME: 1 HOUR

I've always loved looking at all the different designs on sardine tins. Sardines might be a super stinky food, but boy do they come in such pretty packaging!

This sardine tin, however, will hold toothpicks and not stinky fish. It'll also be a great gift for your friend who likes canned fish (or at least the gorgeous tins they come in).

**SUPPLIES**

Canvas mat (optional)

Plastic or acrylic rolling pin

½ lb [230 g] air-dry clay

X-Acto knife

Scoring and slipping tools of your choice (see page 34)

Rounded sculpting tool

Small round-edge paintbrush

Acrylic paint

Toothpicks

Acrylic varnish

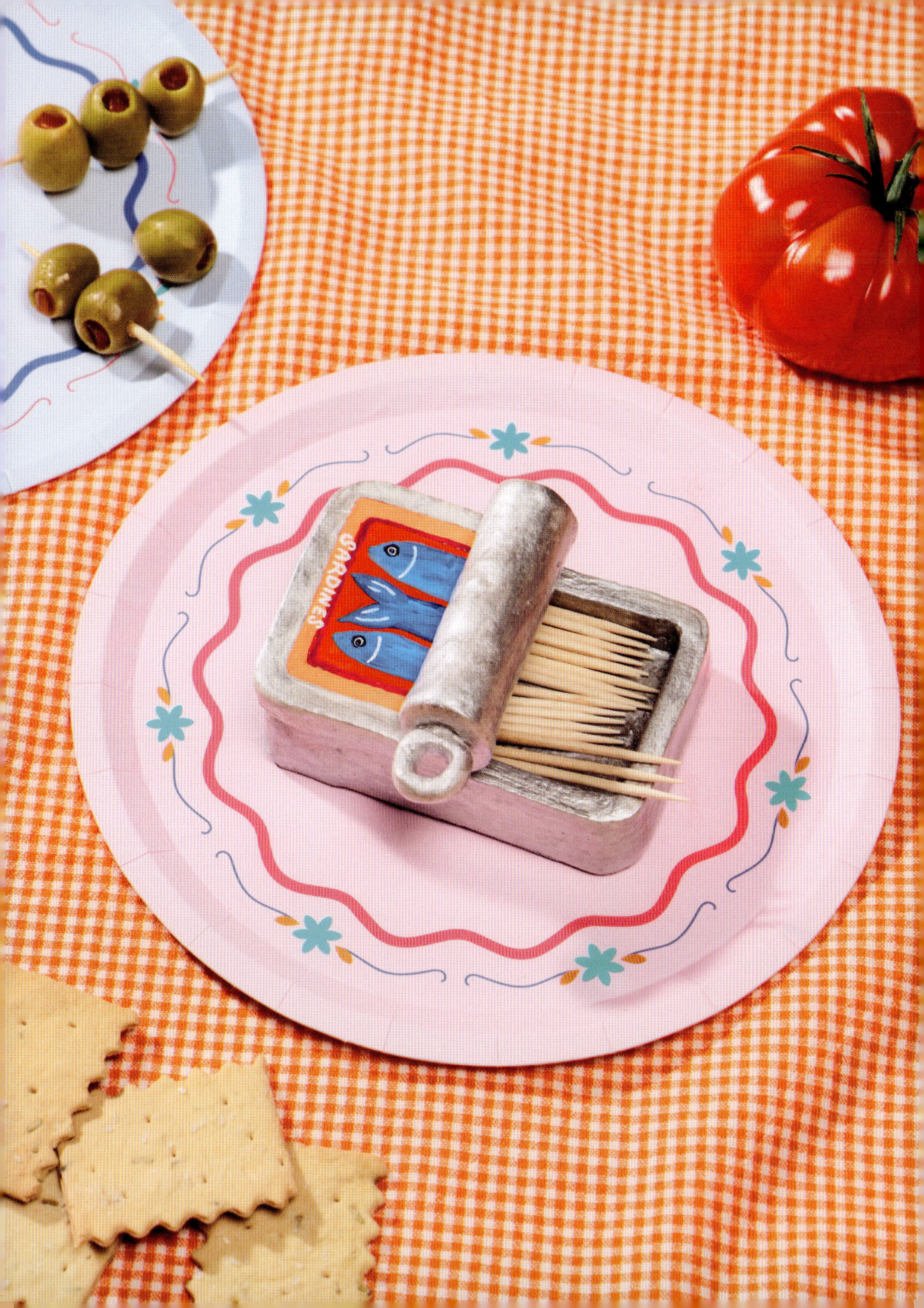
SARDINES

1. On a canvas mat or a clean and flat surface, use the rolling pin to roll the clay out to a ½ in [13 mm] thickness. With the X-Acto knife, cut out two 3½ by 2½ in [9 cm by 6 cm] rectangles with rounded corners.

2. With an X-Acto knife, cut out a ribbon that is ½ in [13 mm] wide and long enough to wrap around the perimeter of one of the rectangles. Score a border about ½ in [13 mm] around the edge of one of the rectangles (see page 34). Add slip and lay the ribbon, edge-side down, along the scored edge. With the rounded sculpting tool, blend the two pieces together to form the walls of the tin, and smooth out any cracks on the bottom and sides.

**3** Grab the second rectangle and, with your fingers, start rolling one end of the clay into itself. Stop rolling halfway—this is the peeled-back lid of the sardine tin.

**4** Roll out a small, thin clay rope and make a loop. Attach this loop to the rolled-out portion of the sardine lid to make it look like the wire that allows for the lid to be wound up in an actual can of sardines. Let the sardine can and lid dry for 24 to 48 hours (follow the instructions on the package of the air-dry clay).

Once the clay is completely dry, paint a little label on the lid and sides of the tin. Alternatively, you can print out a label and glue it in place onto the lid and the sides of the tin. When the paint is dry, add toothpicks to the inside, place the lid back on, and you're done! Brush the tin with a light coat of varnish to make your project more durable.

# A Gifting Guide

The way you gift your handmade crafts can be just as important as the gift itself. Here are some tips for how to make the most of your gifting moment with your bestie:

- **Make a handmade card to go with your gift:** Keep the handmade theme going with a quick and simple card. All you need to do is fold a small piece of craft paper in half, draw some cute shapes on the outside, and write a sweet sentiment on the inside. Or simply make a Funky Bookmark (page 62) and write a note on it.

- **Pair it with some things they can use the craft with:** Think a fancy candle to go with your Cowboy Boot Matchbox with Cowboy Hat Striker (page 82), some pretty actual tinned fish with the Sardine Tin Toothpick Holder (page 92), or a cute little necklace inside of the Strawberry Trinket Dish (page 40).

- **Making a bunch of little crafts for your gift? Make a little gift basket:** In a small basket (find some at your local thrift store) place some shredded paper to create the base. Nestle your gifts on top and add in any store-bought elements (like snacks, cards, etc.). Be sure that your handmade gifts are front and center in the basket since they're the pièce de résistance. Place the whole basket inside a sheer fabric bag or plastic gift bag and seal the top with some ribbon.

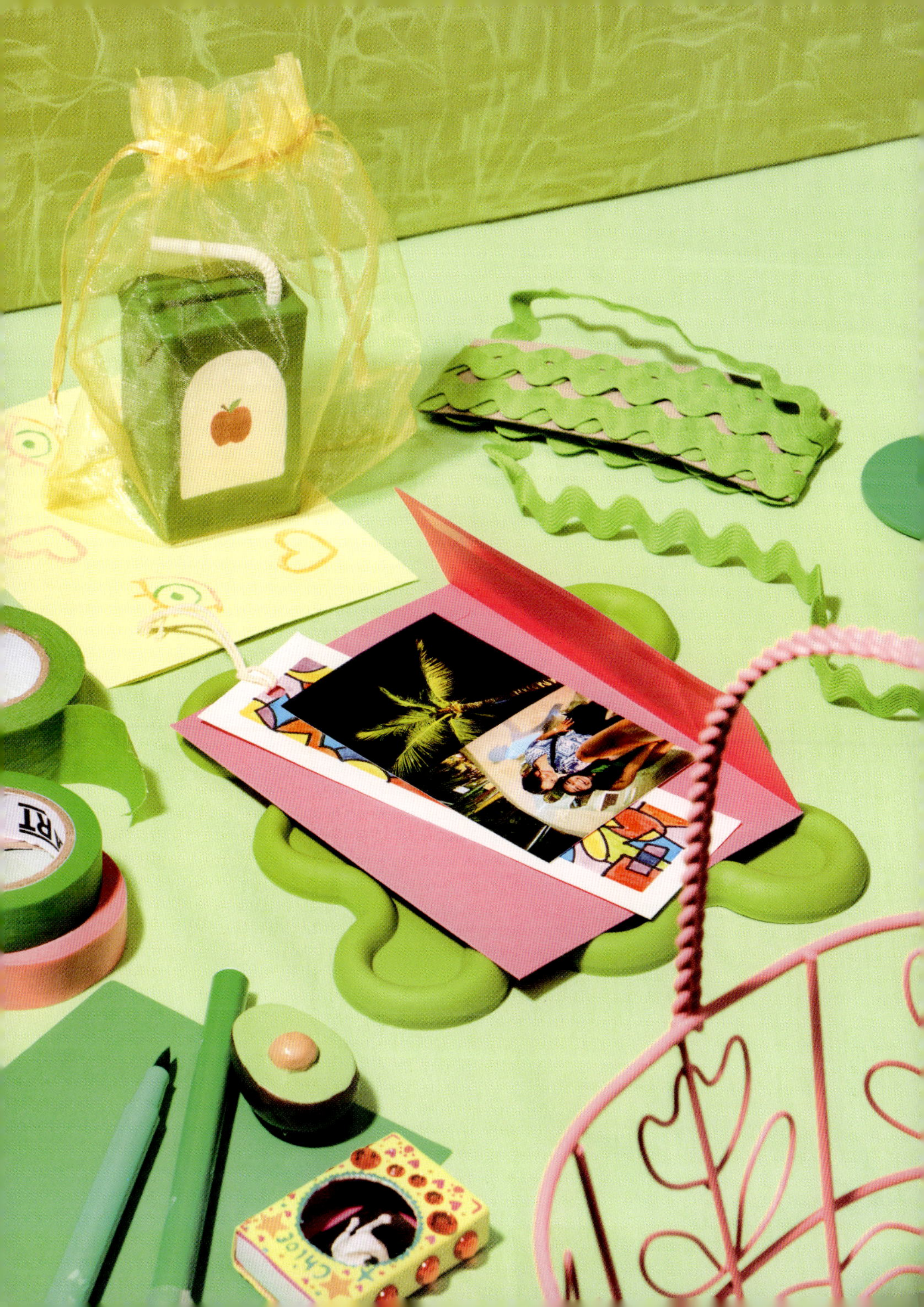
Chloe

# Star Tealight Candle Holder

CRAFTING TIME: 25-35 MINUTES

What's cuter than tealights? This is the perfect gift for that friend who likes to have a tranquil ambiance in their space. The craft itself is super simple, which means you can make a multitude of these lil guys—they would make adorable party favors.

Even if you're not familiar with air-dry clay, this project is beginner friendly, and it'll allow for your creativity to light from within. Get it? Because it's a candle? Haaa . . . OK, I'll stop with the corny jokes. For now.

Like many other crafts in this book, this one is perfect for a group activity.

## SUPPLIES

Canvas mat (optional)

Plastic or acrylic rolling pin

1 lb [455 g] air-dry clay

Large star cookie cutter

Fettling knife

Clay sponge

Ruler or tape measure

Tealights

Scoring and slipping tools (see page 34), preferably an X-Acto knife and small paintbrush

Rounded sculpting tool

Paintbrushes

Acrylic paint

Acrylic varnish

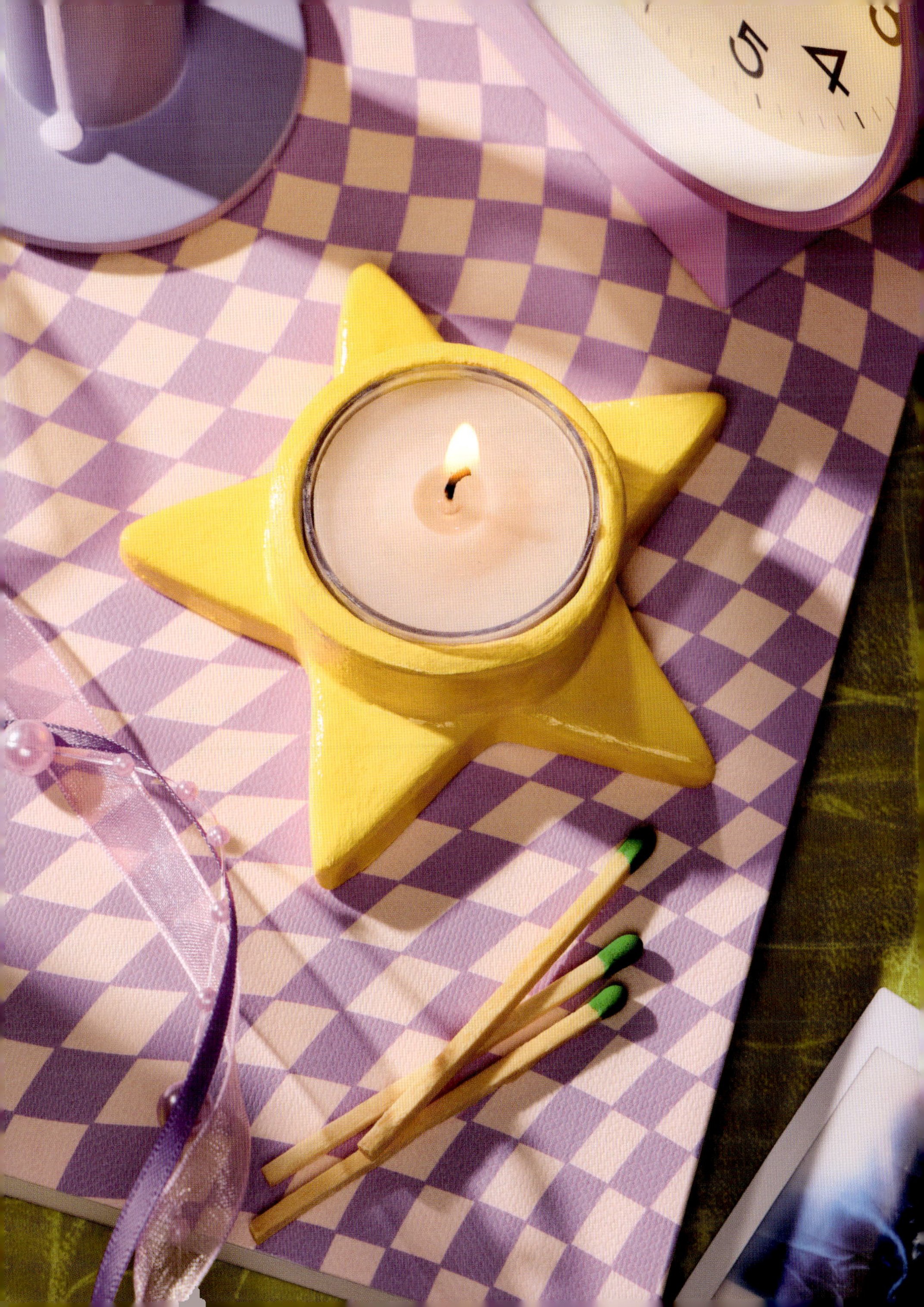

1 On a canvas mat or a clean and flat surface, use the rolling pin to roll half of the clay out to a ½ in [13 mm] thickness. Press the cookie cutter gently into the clay to leave an imprint, then use the fettling knife to cut out the star shape. **Tip:** If you don't have a star-shaped cutter, no worries! Trace or print out a star shape to use as a stencil and use the fettling knife to cut around it. Use a dampened clay sponge to smooth out the rough edges.

2 Using a ruler or tape measure, measure the height of your tealight. Roll out the remaining slab of clay so that it is ¼ in [6 mm] thick. Cut out a ribbon that is 5 in [13 cm] long. The height of the ribbon should match the height of your tealight. Place the tealight right in the center of the clay star and press it gently into the clay. This will leave a slight imprint so you can see where to place the ribbon.

**3** Using an X-Acto knife and a small paintbrush, score and slip along the outside of the candle imprint left on the star and on the bottom side of the ribbon (see page 34). Place the ribbon vertically (¼ in [6 mm] side down) slightly outside of the imprinted circle to make a pocket for the candle that is a little bit wider than the candle itself. (The clay shrinks while drying so this will ensure your candle still fits neatly inside when done.) Use your fingers and the rounded sculpting tool to blend the two pieces together. Blend the two ribbon ends into each other to create a perfectly round pocket for the candle.

**4** Place the tealight inside the pocket and leave it there during the drying process. Let the candle holder dry for 24 to 48 hours (follow the instructions on the package of the air-dry clay).

Once the clay is completely dry, it's ready to be painted. Once the paint is dry, brush the holder with a light coat of varnish to make your project more durable.

# Vintage Magazine Collage Frame

CRAFTING TIME: 30-45 MINUTES

When it comes to making collages, it's all about experimentation and the process of seeing what looks good together. It's the ultimate creative exercise, especially for beginners. You can find vintage magazines, books, and newspapers at thrift stores and antique shops—or print out vintage images.

When making a collage for a friend, try to find things that capture their personality. Also look for other creative elements to elevate the collage itself, like cool fonts to spell out their name. Or maybe cut out a picture of their favorite flower from a magazine. Your using vintage newspapers and magazines to make something modern like a collage frame will definitely be one of the coolest gifts your besties will receive.

### SUPPLIES

**Upcycled plain picture frame (frame must be at least 1½ in [4 cm] wide)**

**Masking tape**

**Newspaper**

**Scissors**

**Vintage magazines, newspapers, or printed-out images**

**Small flat-head paintbrush**

**Craft glue or glue stick**

**Clear, paper-safe sealant spray (like Mod Podge)**

**Lightweight embellishments of choice (like buttons, beads, ribbons, and bows)**

**Silicone glue (like E6000) or a hot-glue gun**

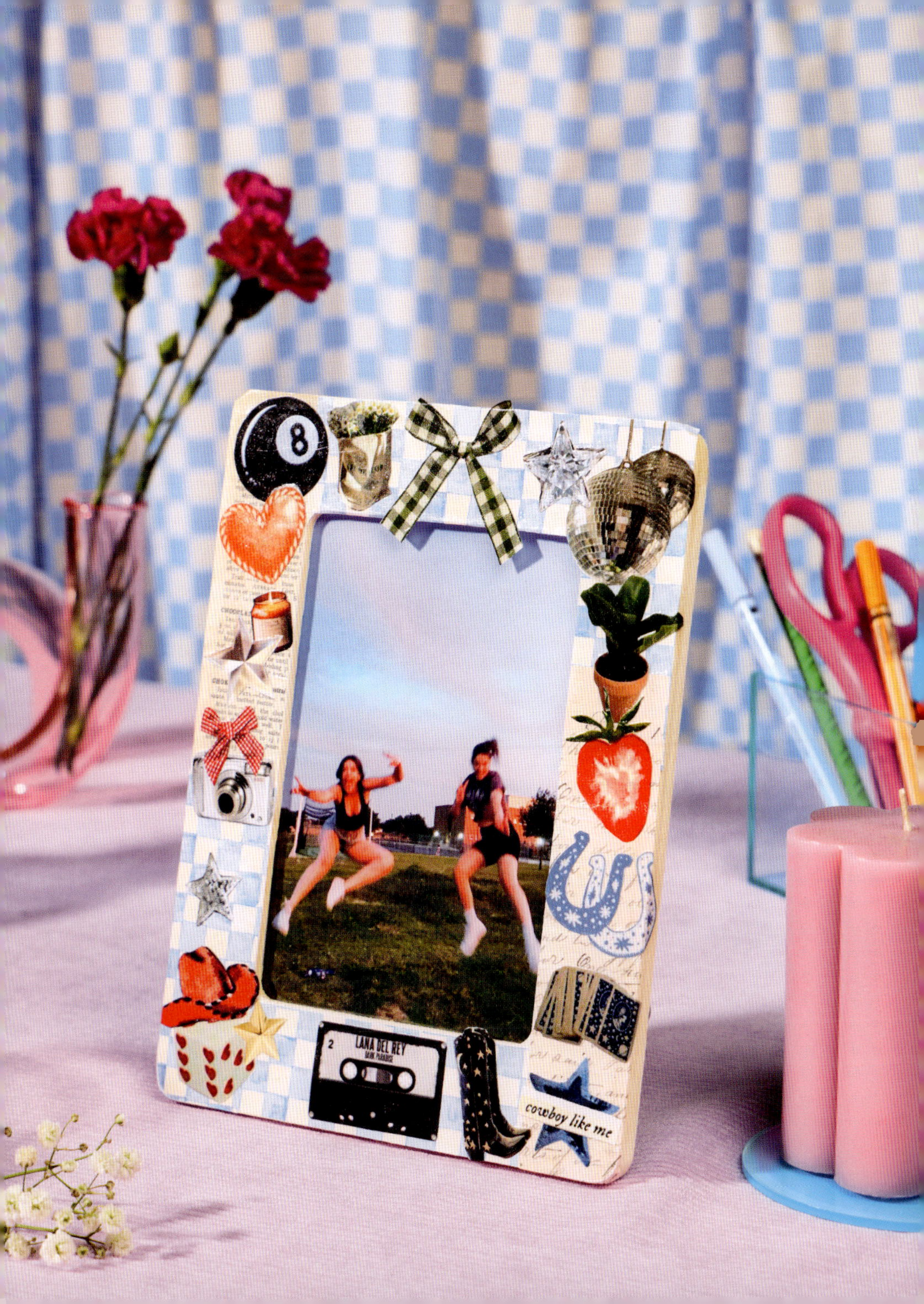
2
LANA DEL REY
cowboy like me

1. Wipe down the frame to make sure the surface is clean and dust-free. Using the masking tape and newspaper, cover the glass or plastic of the frame to protect it from any glue or clear sealant.

2. Cut out lots of images from magazines and newspapers. Arrange your images around the frame to see what placement looks best.

NIFTY GIFTY

**3** Once you've decided on a layout, grab the small flat-head paintbrush and dip it into the craft glue. Apply glue to the back of an image and paste it onto frame. Repeat this step for all the images. Don't be afraid to overlap some pieces. It'll give your collage depth and make it more visually pleasing! Smooth out wrinkles and bubbles as you paste on images. Once everything is in place, allow the glue to dry. Once it's dry, spray the frame with a clear, paper-safe sealant.

**4** Wait for the clear sealant to dry before adding other embellishments like buttons, beads, or ribbon bows using silicone or hot glue.

# Collage Memory Board

CRAFTING TIME: 30–45 MINUTES

SUPPLIES

My favorite thing about memory board collages is that they can encapsulate so many different special moments over the course of a relationship and help you put it all in one place. Whether you're making an anniversary gift for your significant other or a Christmas gift for your sister, the possibilities for this gift are endless. I made this specific memory collage for my sister and compiled some of my favorite memories I have with her and other cute embellishments that I thought would go well with everything else.

If you don't know where to start when making this craft, I suggest gathering all of the sentimental things you have that remind you of the person you're making it for. Let's say you're making this super-thoughtful collage for your significant other. Gather *allll* of the sentimental memorabilia you've collected since you started dating. Try incorporating some of these sentimental things into the collage to make a very heartfelt gift your partner will cherish.

Scissors

Foam board, poster board, or sturdy cardboard

Inspirational images and materials: magazines, newspapers, scrapbook paper, printed images, photos, or sentimental items like movie tickets, notes, or wristbands

Small flat-head paintbrush

Craft glue

Clear, paper-safe sealant spray (like Mod Podge)

Decorations of choice (like stickers, ribbons, beads, and washi tape)

Silicone glue (like E6000) or a hot-glue gun

NIFTY GIFTY

SO SPECIAL
I YOU
LIVE · LAUGH · LOVE
To: my built in bestie
I love you so much & im so grateful for you!! I thank the universe every day for making you my sister. Love you gr gr!
- your sis
1 coupon
Valid for all of my love
The Garden Book

1. With scissors, cut the board into the desired size. My memory board is 10 by 16 in [25 by 40.5 cm]. Gather all the materials you'd like to incorporate in the collage and arrange them on the board.

2. Once everything looks the way you like, dip the paintbrush into the craft glue and spread a thin layer on the back of the images, then paste them in place.

**3** When everything is glued down, set the board aside and allow it to dry. Once everything is nice and dry, spray the entire collage with the clear, paper-safe sealant.

**4** Wait for the clear sealant to dry before adding other embellishments like buttons, beads, or ribbon bows with silicone or hot glue.

Some more ideas to add to your memory board gift:

→ Sentimental memorabilia like old ticket stubs from concerts or movies you went to together.
→ Dried and pressed flowers from old bouquets.
→ Throwback pictures of when you were little.
→ Postcards, letters, or stickers that remind you of your bestie.

# Embroidered Bag Charm

**CRAFTING TIME: 1 HOUR**

**SUPPLIES**

Having cute little keychains or charms hanging from your purse is such a *charming* way to show off personal style. This DIY gift is perfect for that bestie who is always looking for creative ways to accessorize or add a pop of color to their outfit. Whoever receives this craft from you will report back to tell you how many compliments they've gotten on their new handmade charm.

Yes, this craft does involve a little bit of sewing—please don't run away! I know sewing is intimidating for some, but fear not. I didn't know how to sew not too long ago, but it's so easy, I pinky-promise. Also, learning new skills will expand your hot girl tool kit!

And if your besties don't vibe with bag charms, these crafts double as adorable Christmas tree ornaments!

**Tracing paper**

**Marker**

**Scissors**

**Felt fabric**

**Pencil (use a white gel pen or pencil if the felt is a dark color)**

**Embroidery floss (at least 1 yd [91 cm])**

**Embroidery needle**

**Glass seed beads and bugle beads**

**Ribbon or yarn (about 8 in [20 cm])**

**Hot-glue gun**

**Plush stuffing or Poly-Fil**

How to loop your charm onto a purse strap: Place the charm ribbon perpendicular to purse strap. Feed the felt charm through the ribbon loop leaving the purse strap in between. Tug to tightly secure.

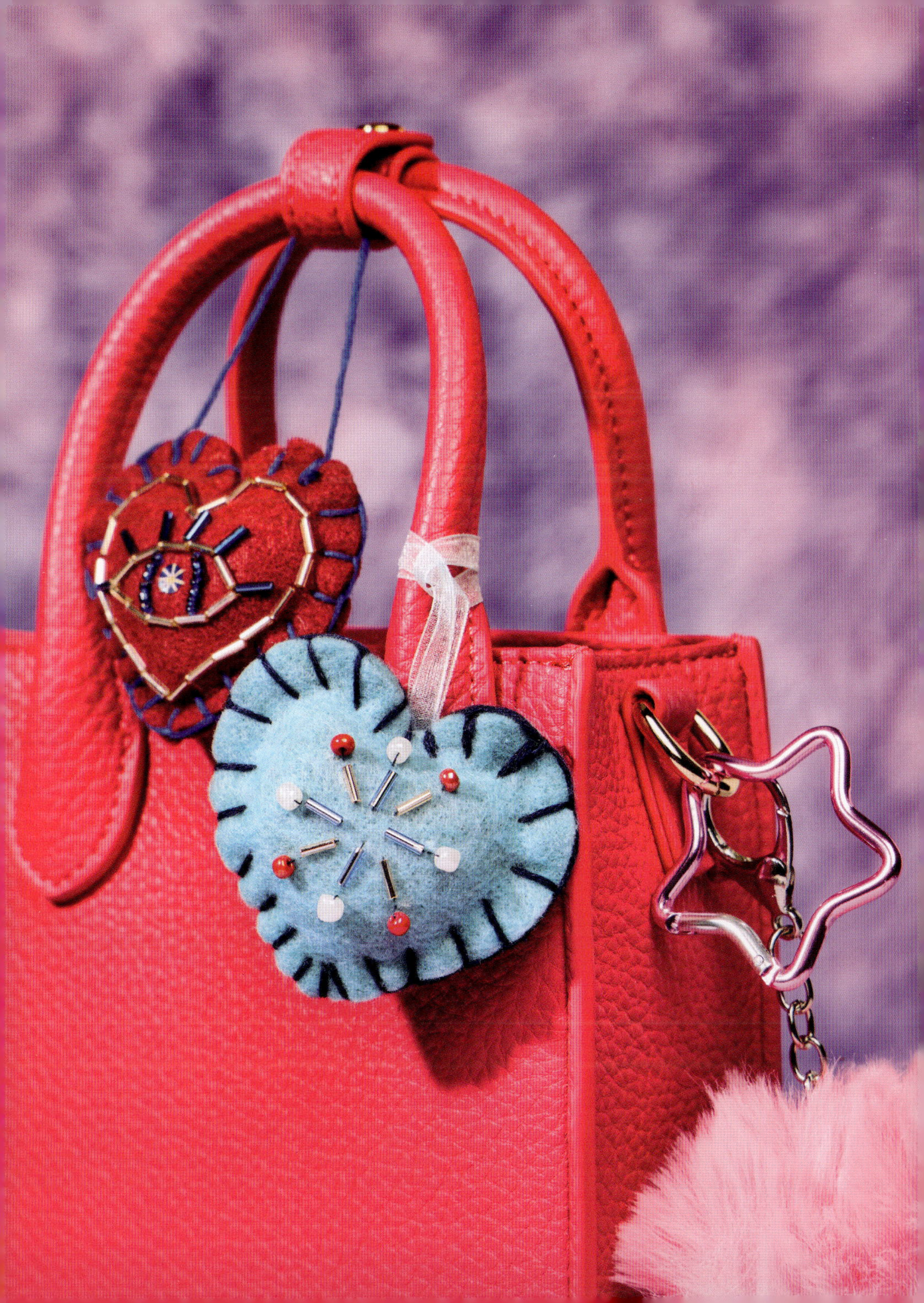

1. Using tracing paper, print and cut out a simple shape that is easy to trace onto the felt fabric. I chose a heart shape and a star, but feel free to use any simple shape. I recommend printing out your shape to be bigger than 3 by 3 in [7.5 by 7.5 cm]. It'll be easier to work with at this size. Using a marker, trace your paper shapes onto the felt fabric. Cut out two of the same shape for each charm you are planning to make (front and back).

2. Use a regular pencil (or a white gel pen or pencil if the felt is a dark color) to sketch a pattern or design of your choosing onto the front piece of your felt shape. This will be the guideline for where to embroider your beads. If you do not want to add a specific design, feel free to embroider beads on randomly, kind of like sprinkles on a cookie.

NIFTY GIFTY

**3** Using your embroidery floss and needle, begin to stitch on the beads. Poke through the back side of the felt, pick up a bead or beads with the tip of the needle, poke the needle back through the felt (the front) then pop the needle back through the back and repeat this process until the embroidery looks as desired. Make sure to take your time on this step because once the charm is sewn together, you won't be able to add more beads.

**4** Cut about 8 in [20 cm] of ribbon and fold it in half to create a loop. Hot glue the ends of the ribbon loop to the inside of the back felt piece of the charm. Stack the two felt pieces on top of each other.

**5** Cut about 18 in [46 cm] of embroidery floss and begin sewing the front and back together with a blanket stitch (see page 114). As you start getting close to the last stitch of your charm, make sure you leave a little opening for the stuffing to go into. Carefully push bits of Poly-Fil into that small opening. Once the charm is stuffed to the desired amount, continue your blanket stitch to close up the charm.

## HOW TO

# Create a Blanket Stitch

Thread a needle and knot the end of the thread (the knot is what secures the start of the blanket stitch). Lift up the front piece of felt or fabric slightly and poke the needle through the back of only the front piece.

Pull the thread all the way through until it's stopped by the knot. Now, poke the needle through both pieces of felt just below the first hole you created. Pull the thread through—now there should be a straight bar of thread.

Hook the needle through the top of the stitch to ensure the stitch stays straight, then pull the thread all the way through. Now you're ready to make the blanket stitch all the way around your project.

cont'd →

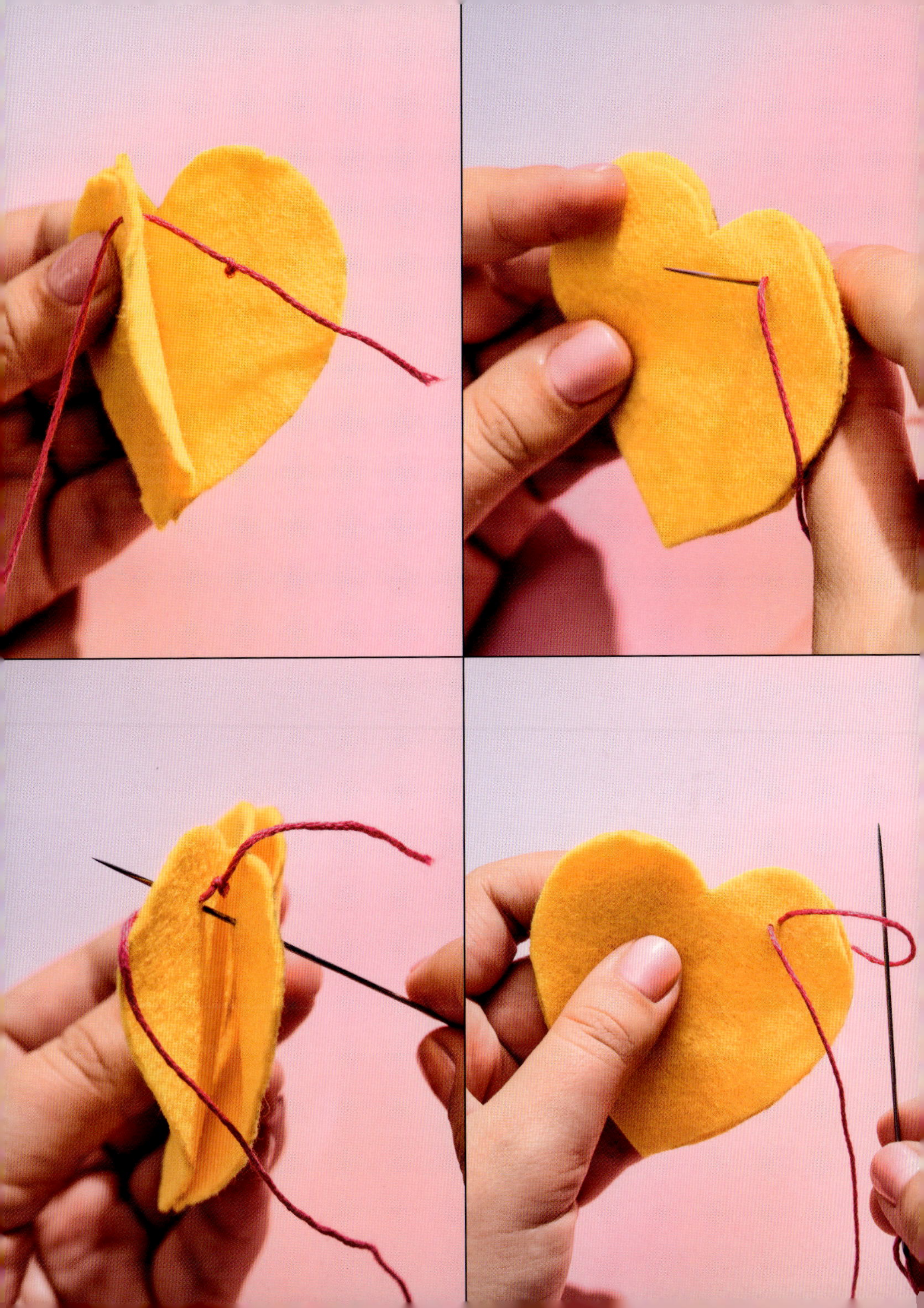

Poke the thread ¼ in [6 mm] away from the very first hole that was created along the edge. Pull the thread through almost all the way, leaving a small loop, then feed the needle through the loop and pull. Repeat this until your project is close to being sealed.

Remember to leave about 1 in [2.5 cm] of open space to be able to fill your project with stuffing (if needed). Once the final blanket stitch is completed, hook the needle twice through the very first stitch made to secure the stitch in place. Create a knot with the final hook and you're done!

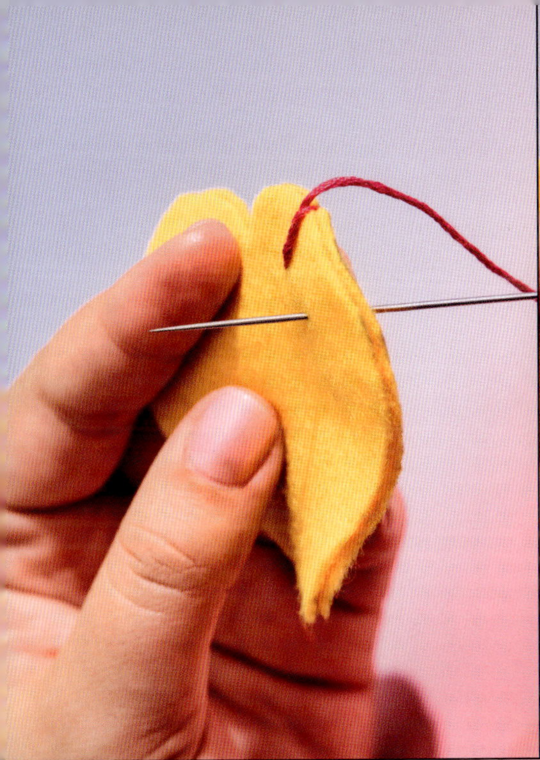
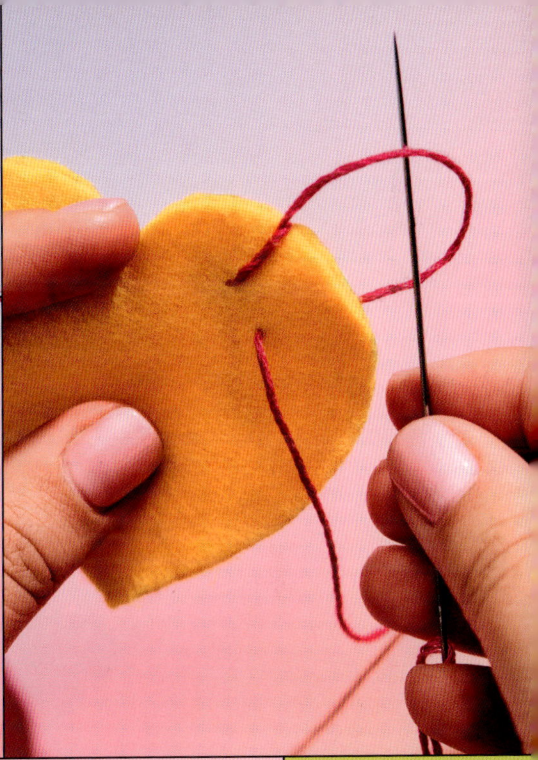
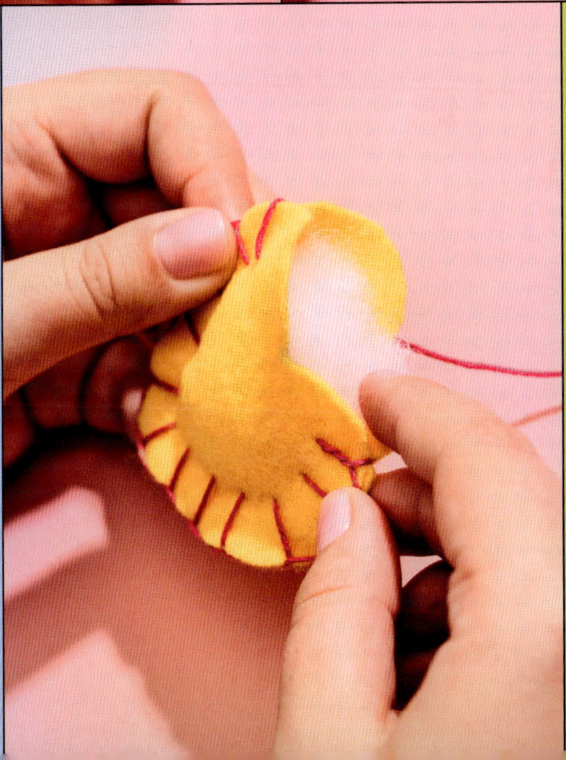

# Beaded Lampshade

CRAFTING TIME: 45-55 MINUTES

I'm so excited to show you how to make this beaded lampshade, but before we get started, I need to make one thing clear: I do *not* want you burning your house down. Please do not use plastic beads, if possible, and if you do, please use an LED bulb. OK, thanks!

We don't want this DIY craft to turn into that one episode of *iCarly* where her brother, Spencer, burns Carly's room down because he made her a gummy bear lampshade for her birthday. I'm sure your bestie will appreciate you not burning down her entire room.

I honestly think this is the most unique craft so far—it's also the most time-consuming. But it's worth the time, I promise! It'll also give you an excuse to binge your favorite show.

Since this is an upcycled craft, our lamps will not be exactly the same, but that's OK! The process is the same, and your lamp will look fantastic. Once it's done, you can see your hard work shining right in front of you, literally.

### SUPPLIES

**Thrifted or upcycled lamp with wire-frame lampshade**

**Scissors**

**Ruler or tape measure**

**Wire cutters**

**22-gauge jewelry beading wire**

**Beads (glass or stone—any material that won't catch fire)**

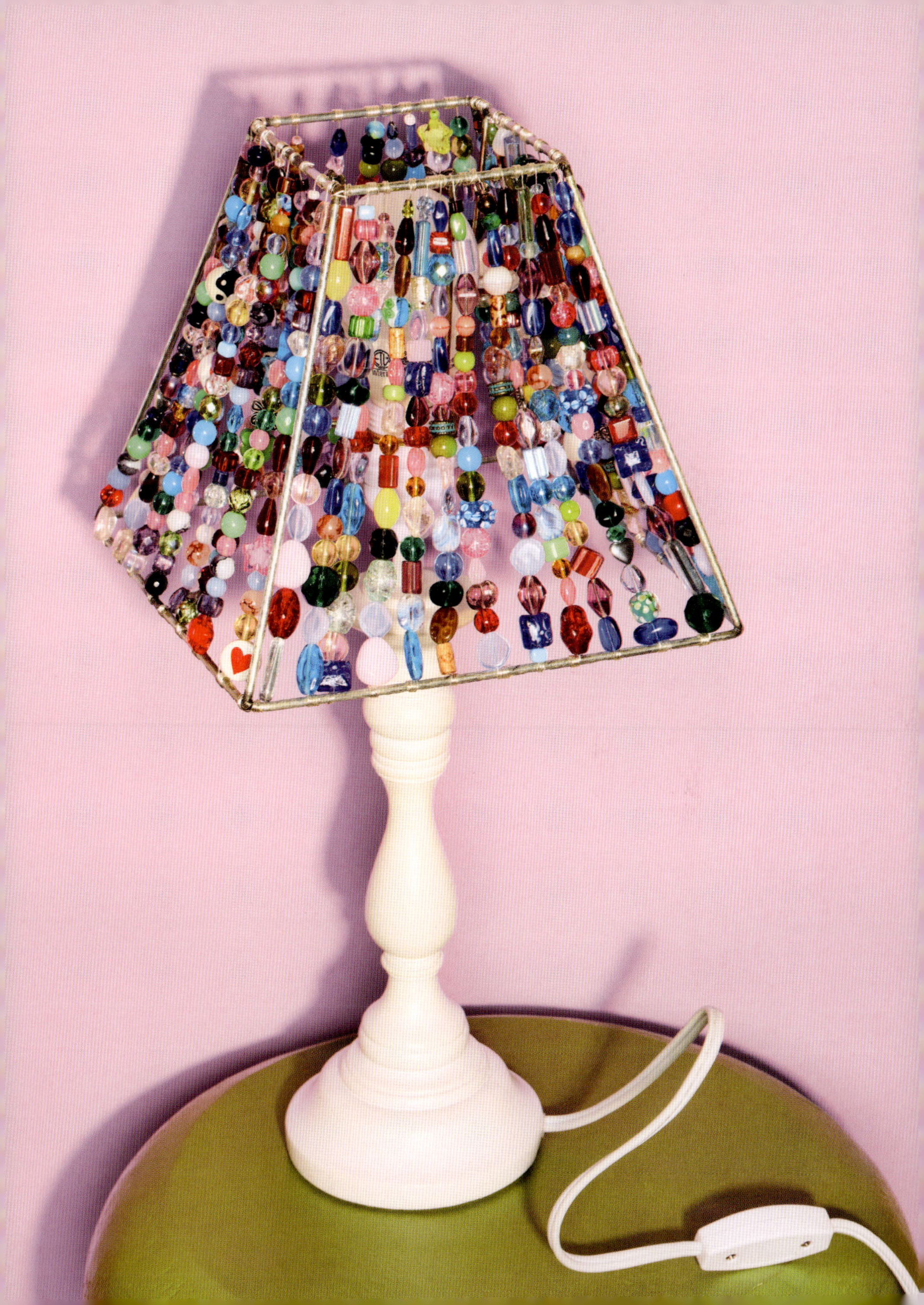

1. Remove the lampshade from the lamp and cut off any fabric that is on the lampshade to reveal the bare wire cage. Set this aside. Use the ruler to measure the distance between the top metal wire circle and the bottom one. This will help determine how long the bead strands need to be for your specific lampshade.

2. Using wire cutters, cut a piece of wire that is a little bit longer than the required length and twist it to the bottom of the lampshade frame.

**3** Begin stringing beads on the wire. Once the beads reach the top of the lampshade frame, twist off the beading wire to secure the beaded line to the top of the frame.

**4** Repeat this process until the entire lampshade frame is covered with beaded strings.

# Matchbox Shrine

**CRAFTING TIME: 25-30 MINUTES**

This gift is perfect for your bestie who is always obsessed with a celebrity. Think of it as their emotional support matchbox shrine, with their favorite celeb tucked into their purse or pocket wherever they go.

The subject of this cute lil shrine could be anyone, from Miley Cyrus to any of the BTS members, a cartoon character, or even your friend's favorite neighborhood cat.

**SUPPLIES**

Empty matchbox

Paintbrushes

Acrylic paint

X-Acto knife

Printed-out image of subject (make sure it can fit inside the matchbox)

Craft glue or glue stick

Pencil

Decorations of choice (like rhinestones, stickers, and glitter)

Gel pen (optional)

Clear, paper-safe sealant spray (like Mod Podge)

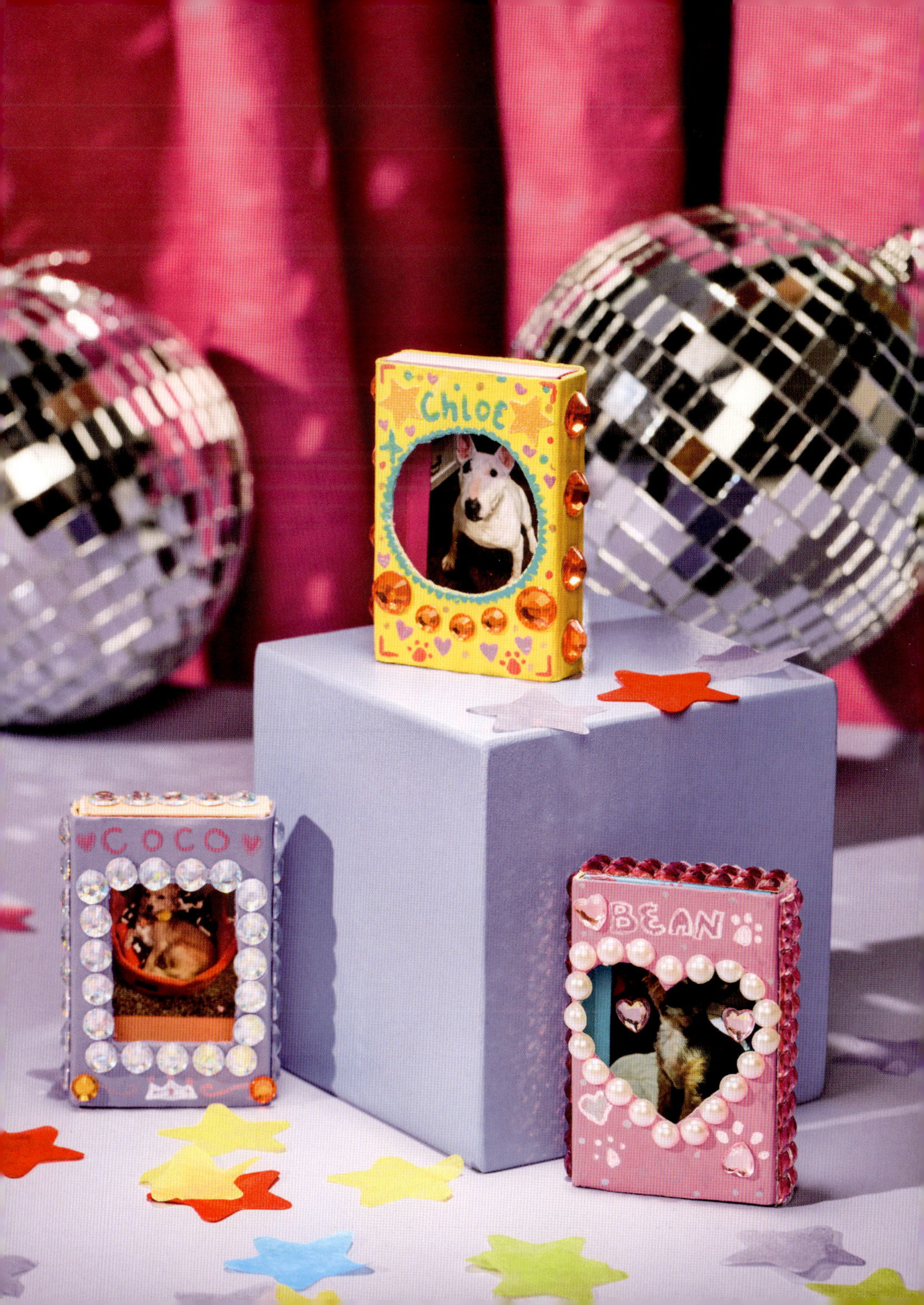
Chloe
COCO
BEAN

1. Pull the inner compartment of the matchbox completely out of the outer shell. Take the outer shell of the matchbox and paint the outside with craft paint. Do not paint the inside of the outer shell. Apply the paint in thin layers to prevent the outer shell from warping. Paint the inside of the inner compartment of the matchbox with a contrasting color from the one used for the outer shell. Or, instead of paint, you can use scrapbooking paper and craft glue to wrap the outer shell and fill in the inner compartment. I find this to be a bit trickier since you have to cut the paper to the size of the matchbox, but it looks just as good!

2. Once both compartments are dry, use the X-Acto knife to cut out the image of the subject of choice you will use for the shrine. Paste this image using craft glue or a glue stick to the inner compartment of the matchbox.

NIFTY GIFTY

**3** Use the pencil to sketch a heart on the front of the outer shell. Using an X-Acto knife, carefully cut along this line to make a heart-shaped window. If a heart is too tricky to cut out, feel free to just do a square or rectangle window.

**4** Now it's time to decorate! I put stick-on pearls along the border of the heart cutout. On the inside, I used a sparkly gel pen to draw hearts and dots to make it look like confetti around the photo. After you're happy with the decorations, spray both parts of the matchbox shrine separately with a clear, paper-safe sealant. Once everything is dry, slide the inner compartment into the outer shell of the box. The photo you pasted inside should peak through the heart-shaped window!

# Fake Cake Gift Box

**CRAFTING TIME: 45–55 MINUTES**

**SUPPLIES**

Sometimes cakes are way too pretty to cut into. It's honestly so heartbreaking to see a beautiful cake being cut and gobbled up! This craft is a beautiful cake that will never be destroyed—it'll last forever!

This project is definitely one of the most time-consuming of the bunch. But once you get the hang of creating fake cakes, you won't want to stop. It's such a cute way to commemorate a special occasion—and much more interesting than a gift card.

If I could give this craft to anyone right now, I would give it to you! You've stuck with me through this wonderful craft-making journey. I think you deserve a beautiful little fake cake (and a real one too).

**Circular wooden, cardboard, or paper-mache gift box**

**Paintbrushes**

**Acrylic paint**

**Joint compound or lightweight spackle**

**2 small plastic cups**

**Plastic frosting bags and piping tips (open star-shaped tips size 18 and 21)**

**2 tall plastic cups**

**Plastic spoons**

**Fake cherry (optional)**

**Mini cake stand (optional)**

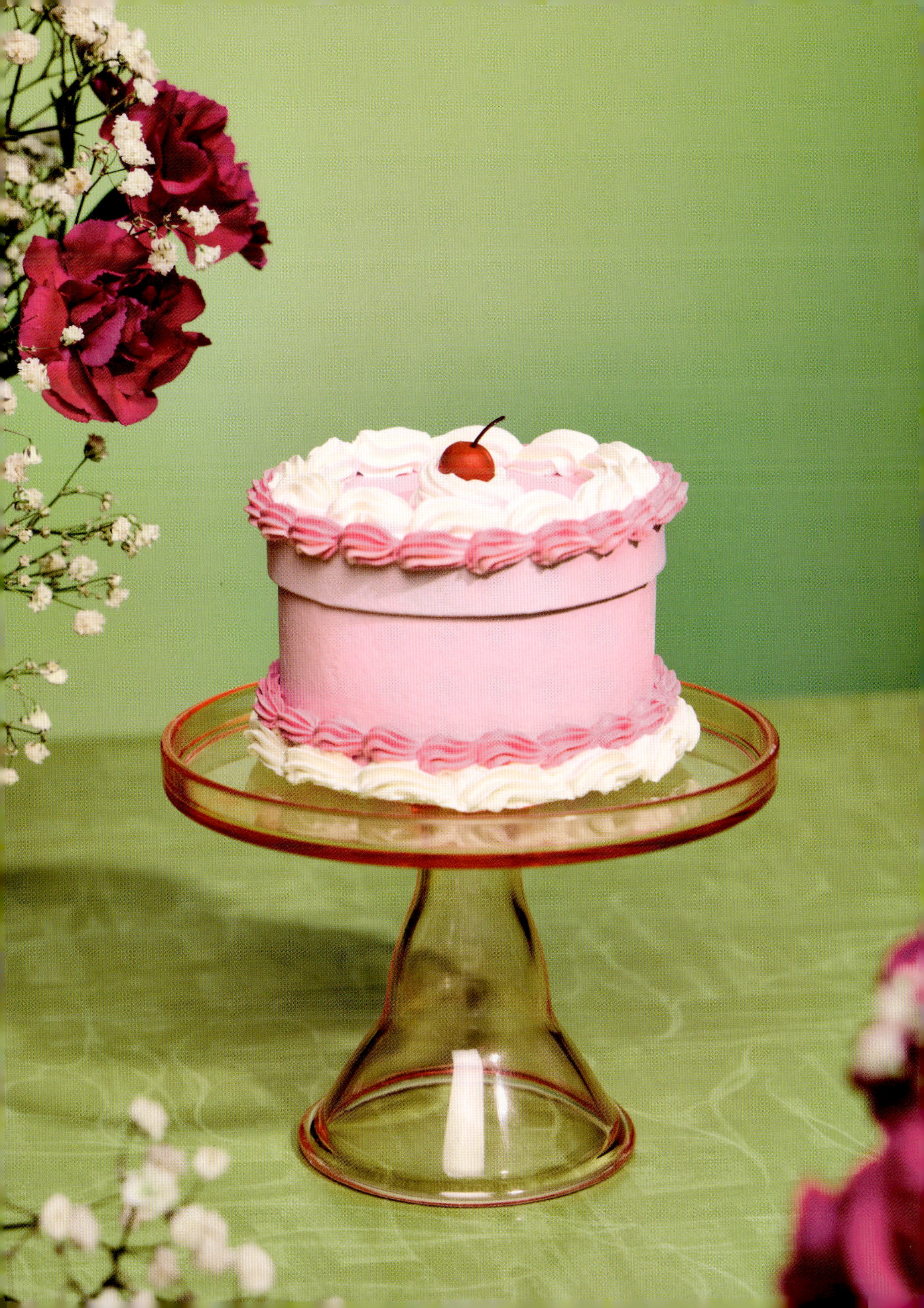

NIFTY GIFTY 128

1. Paint the outside of the gift box with your paint color of choice. (I used pastel pink.) Take off the lid and paint it separately if needed. Set it aside to dry.

2. Scoop 2 heaping tablespoons of the joint compound or lightweight spackle into two small plastic cups (2 tablespoons in each cup). This will be the fake cake frosting. Use the acrylic paint to add color to both of the cups of spackle. I added pink paint in one and white in the other. **Tip:** Even though the spackle is already white, adding white craft paint makes it a brighter shade of white.

3. Prepare the plastic frosting bags with piping tips. For the white frosting bag, I used a size 21 tip, and for the pink bag, I used the size 18 piping tip. Secure the tips in place. Place the frosting bags inside the tall plastic cups, tip down. Fold the edges of the bags over the rims of the cups so they cuff around them. This is one of my favorite piping bag methods because it ensures that you fill the bag with the icing without the hassle and mess. Scoop all the fake icing from the small plastic cups into the piping bags with the plastic spoons. Once both bags are filled, uncuff the tops of the frosting bags from the large plastic cups and twist the tops of the bags. Push the fake icing down toward the piping tip.

cont'd →

**4** Begin to pipe the white icing (or whatever color icing is in the bag with the bigger star tip) along the top edge of the gift box lid.

**5** Repeat this same piping pattern around the bottom of the box. Use the pink frosting (star piping tip 18) to pipe along the outer border of the white frosting (almost on the side edge of the gift box lid).

**6** On the bottom of the gift box, pipe the pink frosting directly on top of the white. Switch back to the white frosting, and pipe a circle on the top of the gift box.

**7** Before the spackle hardens, place a fake cherry or any other decor on top of the frosting circle, if using. Leave the cake somewhere safe to dry. Gift on a mini cake stand, if you have one.

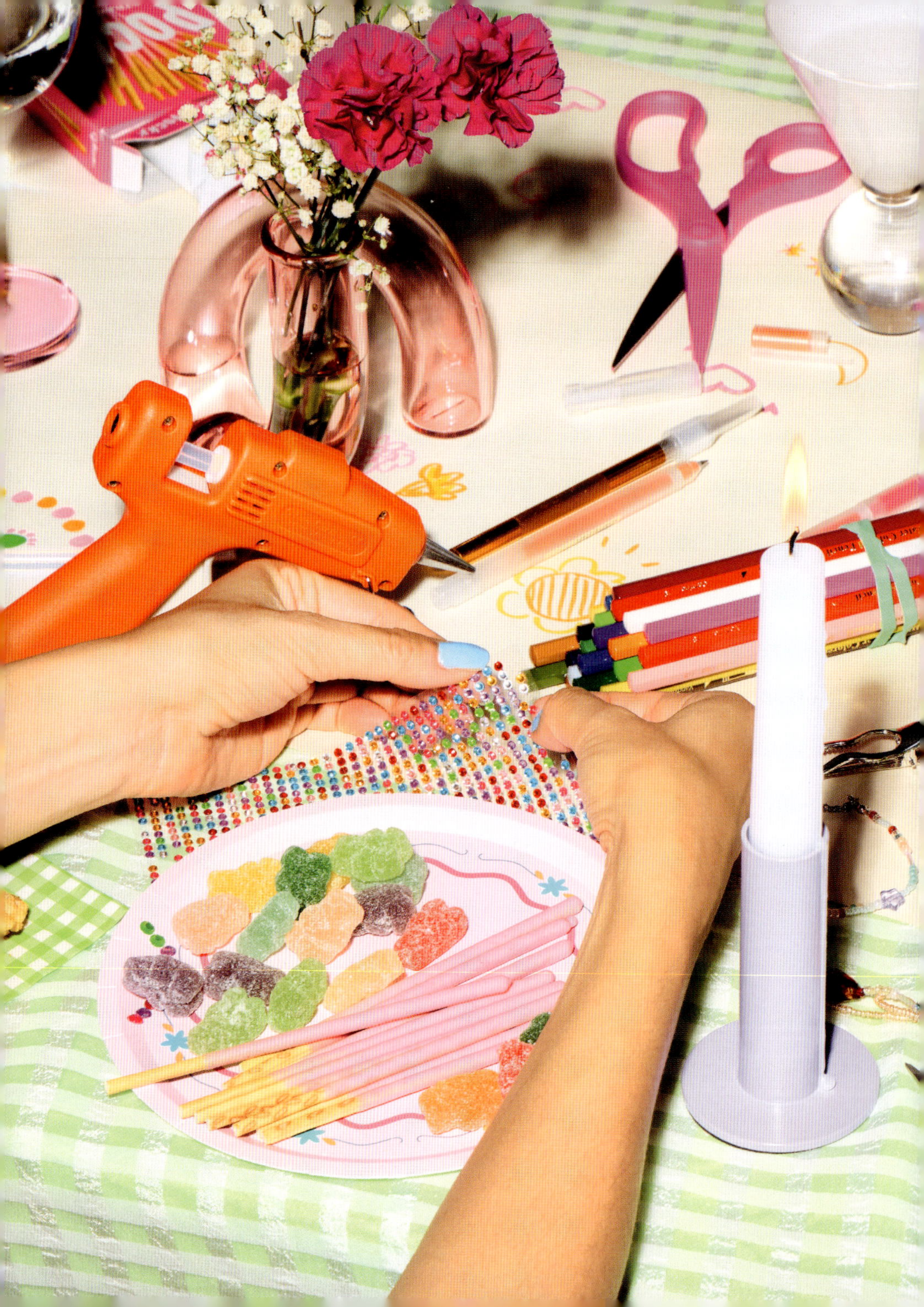

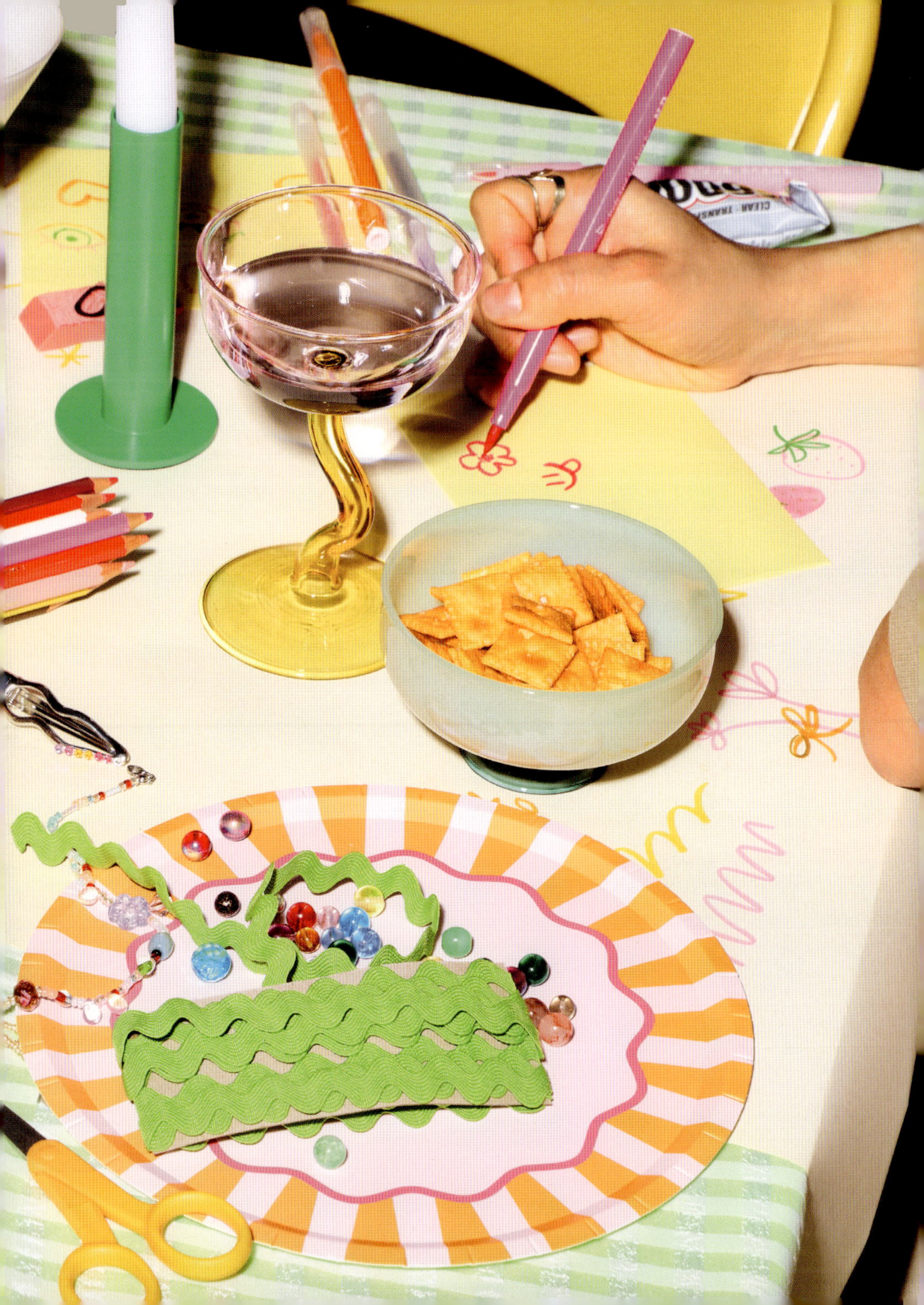
CLEAR

# Acknowledgments

This book couldn't have been possible without the unwavering support of my friends and family: Angel, Lidia, Angelica, Shida, and Haley. I love you all sooooo much. Thank you for being my cheerleaders and believing in me.

Extra special thanks to my entire Chronicle Books team. Thank you to my editors Dena, Alex, and Karah for guiding me through this book-making journey. I will forever be grateful for this opportunity!

Thank you to every single person who has liked my silly crafting videos online. I promise to post more since I have more time because this book is now published (hehe). Love you all!

ACKNOWLEDGMENTS

**NIFTY GIFTY**

# About the Author

**Alexa Pedrero** is a Mexican American artist, content creator, and first-time author. She has always been passionate about creating art and, more recently, has turned to making her art into gifts.

You can find even more of her cute and quirky crafts at @Lauraleii on TikTok and @Lauraleii.art on Instagram.

# Index

## A
adhesives, 10
Avocado Magnet, 76

## B
Bag Charm, Embroidered, 110–13
beading
  Beaded Lampshade, 118–21
  tools and supplies, 11
Bejeweled Lighter, 52–55
blanket stitch, 114–17
Bookmarks, Funky, 62–69

## C
Cake Gift Box, Fake, 126–31
Candle Holder, Star Tealight, 98–101
Charm, Embroidered Bag, 110–13

clay, air-dry, 12
clay projects
  Cowboy Boot Matchbox with Cowboy Hat Striker, 82–87
  Fruit Magnets, 74–79
  Juice Box Picture Holder, 28–33
  Mini Clay Floatie, 50–51
  Mini Pool-Shaped Trinket Dish, 44–51
  Mini Trinket Shelf, 36–39
  Mushroom Picture Holder, 22–26
  Sardine Tin Toothpick Holder, 92–95
  Star Tealight Candle Holder, 98–101
  Strawberry Trinket Dish, 40–43
  Sun Incense Holder, 88–91

**clay techniques**
  scoring, 34
  slipping, 34
**clay tools, 12**
**collage**
  Collage Memory Board, 106–9
  Vintage Magazine Collage Frame, 102–5
**Cowboy Boot Matchbox with Cowboy Hat Striker, 82–87**
**crafting night, hosting, 56**
**cutting supplies, 19**

# D

**decoration, 16**
**dishes**
  Mini Pool-Shaped Trinket Dish, 44–51
  Strawberry Trinket Dish, 40–43

# E

**embellishments, 16**
**Embroidered Bag Charm, 110–13**
**Eraser Stamp, 70–73**

# F

**Fake Cake Gift Box, 126–31**
**Floatie, Mini Clay, 50–51**
**Frame, Vintage Magazine Collage, 102–5**

Fruit Magnets, 74–79
Funky Bookmarks, 62–69

## G
Gift Box, Fake Cake, 126–31
gifting tips, 96
glue, 10

## I
Incense Holder, Sun, 88–91

## J
Juice Box Picture Holder, 28–33

## K
Kisses Bookmark, Funky, 69

## L
Lampshade, Beaded, 118–21
Lighter, Bejeweled, 52–55

## M
Magazine Collage Frame, Vintage, 102–5
Magnets, Fruit, 74–79
markers, 16
masking tape, 10
matchboxes
    Cowboy Boot Matchbox, 84–85
    Matchbox Shrine, 122–25
Memory Board, Collage, 106–9
Mini Clay Floatie, 50–51
Mini Pool-Shaped Trinket Dish, 44–51

Mini Trinket Shelf, 36–39
Mint Tin Wallet, 58–61
Mushroom Picture Holder, 22–26

## P

painting supplies, 18
paper, 16
pens, 16
picture holders and frames
   Juice Box Picture Holder, 28–33
   Mushroom Picture Holder, 22–26
   Vintage Magazine Collage Frame, 102–5
**Pool-Shaped Trinket Dish, Mini, 44–51**

## S

Sardine Tin Toothpick Holder, 92–95
scissors, 19
scoring, 34
sealants, 19
selling tips, 80
Shelf, Mini Trinket, 36–39
Shrine, Matchbox, 122–25
slipping, 34
**Stained Glass Bookmark, Funky, 67**
**Stamp, Eraser, 70–73**
**Star Tealight Candle Holder, 98–101**
strawberries
   Funky Strawberry Bookmark, 64
   Strawberry Magnet, 78–79
   Strawberry Trinket Dish, 40–43

Striker, Cowboy Hat, 86–87
Sun Incense Holder, 88–91
supplies, 10–13, 16, 18–19

## T

tools, 10–13, 16, 18–19
Toothpick Holder, Sardine Tin, 92–95
**trinket holders**
   Mini Pool-Shaped Trinket Dish, 44–51
   Mini Trinket Shelf, 36–39
   Strawberry Trinket Dish, 40–43

## V

Vintage Magazine Collage Frame, 102–5

## W

Wallet, Mint Tin, 58–61
Watermelon Magnet, 77

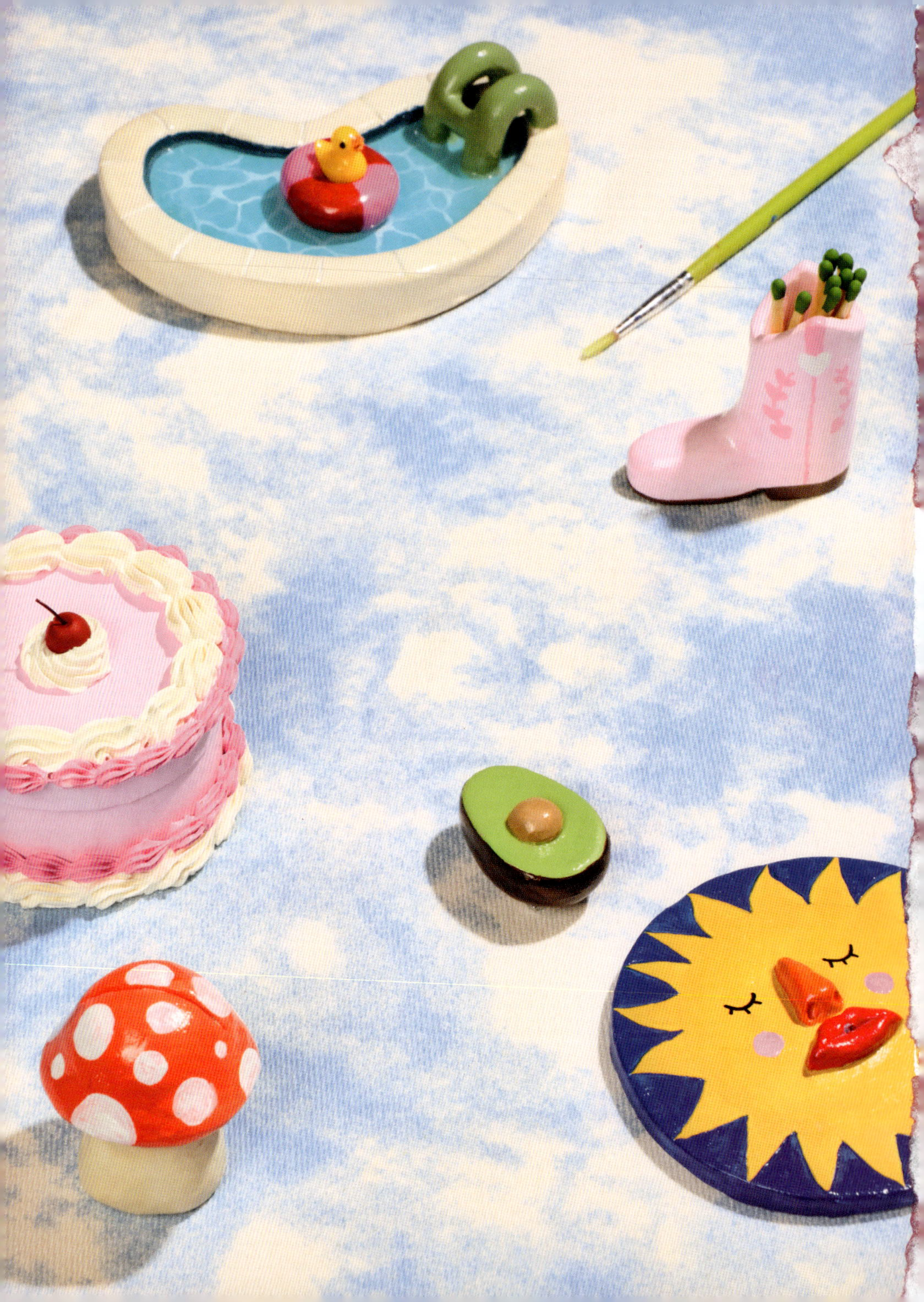

Chronicle Books publishes distinctive books and gifts. From award-winning children's titles, bestselling cookbooks, and eclectic pop culture to acclaimed works of art and design, stationery, and journals, we craft publishing that's instantly recognizable for its spirit and creativity. Enjoy our publishing and become part of our community at www.chroniclebooks.com.

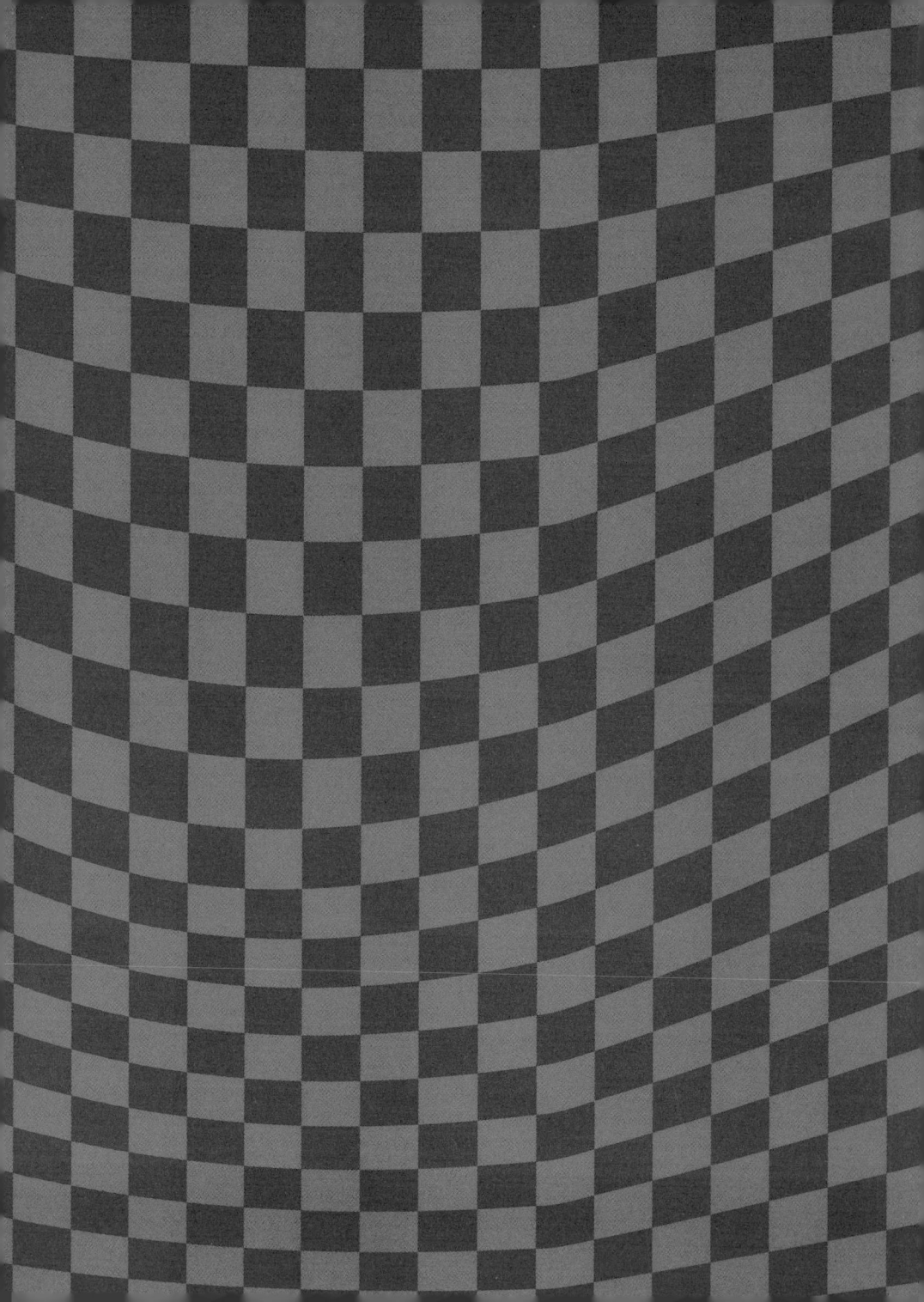